THE WITCH WITHIN, VOLUME 11

MODERN PRACTICAL SPELLS FOR EMPOWERMENT AND PERSONAL GROWTH

CERRIDWEN MAEVE

CONTENTS

INTRODUCTION

From the moment I first felt the stirrings of magic within me, I knew that my path was to share this enchanting world with others. My journey into the heart of witchcraft began on a seemingly ordinary day when a simple garden ritual unexpectedly opened a doorway into a realm of profound transformation and empowerment. This experience ignited a passion within me to delve deeper into the mysteries of witchcraft, not just as a personal refuge but as a potent tool for personal and collective empowerment.

As a practitioner dedicated to empowering women through the mystical arts, I have crafted this book to bridge the ancient wisdom of our ancestors and the pulsating beat of our modern lives. I am committed to demystifying witchcraft, making it accessible and relevant for you, regardless of your background or lifestyle. This book is not just about learning spells—it's about weaving magic into your daily life and reclaiming your power through self-care, creativity, and spiritual growth.

This book is designed to be your companion in exploring practical, adaptable spellwork that honors cultural traditions while embracing modern innovations like digital apps. I aim to guide you in creating a magical practice that is as unique as you are, built on a foundation of ethical principles and safety.

Throughout these pages, I tackle historical and cultural contexts with respect, ensuring that our practice enriches our understanding rather than appropriating from cultures. This commitment to cultural respect helps bridge the gap between curiosity and genuine, informed practice, allowing us to celebrate the diversity within the witchcraft community.

In response to common misconceptions, I want to clarify that witchcraft is not about wielding unchecked power or engaging in dark arts; rather, it's a path of enlightenment, self-discovery, and connection to the natural world. By choosing to pick up this book, you are stepping away from stereotypes and stepping into a circle of empowerment and enlightenment.

The structure of this book is designed to guide you through foundational principles, moving into practical spells and rituals, and finally, helping you integrate these practices into your everyday life. Each chapter builds upon the last, creating a comprehensive guide that will equip you with the tools to transform mundane tasks into magical experiences.

Safety and ethical practices are paramount in my approach to spellcasting. I emphasize these aspects not only to guide you in responsible practice but also to foster a community of practitioners who respect the inherent power and responsibility that comes with wielding the magical arts.

As we embark on this journey together, I invite you to open your heart to the endless possibilities that lie within you. Embrace this opportunity to ignite your inner magic, to grow and transform in ways you never imagined. Let's awaken "The Witch Within" and discover together the profound impact that modern witchcraft can have on our lives.

∽

Welcome to a journey of empowerment, personal growth, and magical discovery. Let the magic begin!

CHAPTER 1
FOUNDATIONS OF MODERN WITCHCRAFT

Wen I first began my path in witchcraft, I was gifted a small, aged book of shadows by a wise woman in my life. As I leafed through the weathered pages filled with notes and spells passed down through generations, I realized that these weren't just recipes or incantations—they were a legacy of responsibility and ethics bound by unseen cords to the past and future. It was a profound reminder that our actions ripple through time and affect more than just our immediate surroundings. This realization forms the cornerstone of this chapter, where we delve into the ethical framework that sustains a healthy, empowering, and respectful magical practice.

1.1 THE ETHICS OF MODERN SPELLCASTING

Understanding Consent

In modern witchcraft, consent isn't just a formality—it's the foundation of ethical spellwork. Obtaining explicit permission from anyone you wish to include in your spells is crucial. This respects their autonomy and honors their free will, which is paramount in all forms of magical practice. Imagine casting a love spell involving a specific person without their consent; such actions can manipulate their feelings, leading to karmic repercussions that affect all involved. Instead, ethical spellwork focuses on spells that invite love into your life without binding a specific person to your will. This approach ensures that your magical workings align with the universal law of respect and are more likely to bring about positive outcomes that cause no harm.

The Threefold Law

Central to many paths in witchcraft is the Threefold Law, which posits that whatever energy you put out into the universe—positive or negative—will return to you threefold. Think of it as the echo of your actions and intentions bouncing back, magnified. This principle serves as a constant reminder to consider the intentions and potential impacts of your spells. Casting a spell out of anger or vengeance, for example, not only harms the target but can also bring thrice the negativity back into your life. Instead, focus on spells that foster positivity and growth—like those for healing, protection, or peace—which can enrich your life and the lives of others in expansive and beneficial ways.

Responsibility in Spellcasting

Wielding magical power comes with significant responsibility. Every spell and ritual should be approached with a clear understanding of its potential consequences. Before casting, it's essential to ask yourself several questions: What are my intentions? Are there potential negative outcomes? How might this affect others? By considering these elements, you ensure that your practices contribute positively to the world and reflect the ethical standards that uphold the integrity of witchcraft. For instance, instead of casting a spell to get a specific job, focus on attracting the right job for you, thus not interfering with others' opportunities and outcomes.

Avoiding Cultural Appropriation

As witchcraft continues to grow in diversity, it's vital to engage with different cultural practices with both respect and sensitivity. Cultural appropriation—borrowing symbols, rituals, or practices from a culture not your own without proper understanding or respect—can lead to misrepresentations and disrespect. To honor the traditions you wish to incorporate, invest time in learning about their historical, cultural, and spiritual contexts. Engage with practitioners within those cultures when possible, and always approach with humility and the intention to honor rather than take. For example, if you're drawn to using sage for smudging, consider the plant's significance to Native American cultures first. Explore alternatives that hold a similar cleansing property, like rosemary or lavender, which might be more aligned with your heritage and local practices, thereby avoiding cultural insensitivity.

Interactive Element: Self-Reflection Exercise

Consider your own practices and jot down answers to these questions:

- Have I ever used elements from other cultures in my spells? Did I research their origins and meanings?
- Do I always seek consent from those involved in my spells?
- How do I ensure that my spellwork adheres to the Threefold Law?

This exercise is designed to help you reflect on and refine your approach to ethical spellcasting, ensuring that your practice is not only powerful but also respectful and responsible. By maintaining a commitment to these ethical standards, you actively contribute to the positive evolution of modern witchcraft, fostering a practice that is inclusive, respectful, and profoundly transformative.

1.2 EMPOWERMENT THROUGH WITCHCRAFT

The transformative power of witchcraft extends far beyond the realms of the mystical and into the very fabric of personal development and empowerment. Through the practice of witchcraft, you tap into ancient wisdom that fosters growth and strength, guiding you to a deeper understanding of your inner self and enhancing your ability to navigate the world with confidence and resilience. The practice of magic becomes a profound journey of self-discovery, where each spell and ritual is not merely an act of will but a step toward becoming the most empowered version of yourself.

At its core, Witchcraft is about connection—connection to oneself, the Earth, and the web of life that surrounds us. This connection begins with self-awareness and extends outward, influencing every aspect of our lives. By engaging in personal growth through magic, you're essentially setting the stage for a life transformed by your own power and intention. Consider a simple grounding spell, which involves visualizing roots extending from your feet deep into the Earth. This not only promotes a sense of stability and presence but also subtly enhances your self-esteem as you become more attuned to your environment and your place within it. Each spell, no matter how small, builds a foundation of confidence and empowerment, brick by brick, until you stand strong, rooted in your own power.

The role of self-care in this empowering practice cannot be overstated. In a world that often demands that women put others first, claiming time and space for your own well-being is a radical act of self-empowerment. Self-care spells and rituals are tools that remind you of your worth and teach you to nurture not just your physical body but your spirit and mind as well. A simple ritual like crafting a self-care jar—filled with items that symbolize love, relaxation, and protection, such as rose petals for love, lavender for relaxation, and black tourmaline for protection—serves as a physical manifestation of your commitment to self-care. Each time you see or hold this jar, you're reminded of the importance of looking after yourself, reinforcing the idea that self-care is essential to personal empowerment.

Spellcasting also offers a unique pathway to building confidence and resilience. Regular practice of spells and rituals reinforces your belief in your own abilities and helps cultivate a positive self-image. For instance, a spell to enhance personal courage, possibly before a significant life change or challenge, involves speaking affirmations aloud while holding a courage-enhancing stone like a carnelian. This ritual not only sets a powerful intention but also embeds these affirmations into your consciousness, gradually building a reservoir of confidence that you can draw upon when faced with future challenges. Over time, the regular practice of such spells shapes you into a more confident and resilient individual, fully empowered to meet life head-on.

Moreover, witchcraft's interconnection with modern feminist movements offers a framework for understanding and addressing the challenges faced by women and marginalized groups. The empowerment aspect of witchcraft aligns beautifully with feminism's goals of equality and justice, offering both symbolic and practical tools for resistance and self-affirmation. In communities where women's voices have traditionally been marginalized, witchcraft serves as a means of reclaiming power and agency. It provides a spiritual framework for understanding one's power and practical tools to assert that power. For example, a group spell on International Women's Day, focusing on empowerment and solidarity, can be a powerful way for women to connect, support each other, and reinforce their commitment to feminist principles.

In this way, witchcraft transcends the boundaries of mere personal development. It becomes a transformative force that not only empowers the individual practitioner but also has the potential to reshape communities. It encourages a deep, personal empowerment that radiates outward, influencing every aspect of your life and touching everyone around you. Through the thoughtful practice of spells and rituals, you not only change yourself; you change your world.

I.3 WITCHCRAFT IN THE DIGITAL AGE

In this digital era, the ancient practices of witchcraft are evolving in exciting new ways that make the craft more accessible and integrated into our daily lives. Technology, when used thoughtfully, can enhance the practice of witch-craft, making it easier to access information, connect with like-minded individuals, and even enhance the rituals themselves. Let's explore how modern witches can harness the power of technology to deepen their practice and expand their magical knowledge.

Integrating Technology

The integration of technology into witchcraft opens up a myriad of tools that can enhance the magical experience.

Consider, for instance, the use of apps that track moon phases. These apps can be invaluable in planning rituals that correspond with lunar energies, ensuring you're working with the right energy at the right time. Digital altars can also play a significant role, especially for those who may need more space or privacy for a physical altar. A digital altar can be a designated folder on your computer or a private page on a social media platform where you gather images, chants, spells, and inspirations that resonate with your spiritual practice. This can be particularly empowering for individuals who are still in the "broom closet" (a term used within the witchcraft community to refer to those who keep their practices secret from friends, family, or coworkers), allowing them to practice discreetly without having to forego the sacred space an altar provides.

Online Communities

The role of online communities in witchcraft cannot be overstated. These digital gathering places offer support, education, and a sense of belonging that can be hard to find offline, especially for those living in areas where witchcraft is still misunderstood or stigmatized. Platforms like Reddit, Discord, and specialized forums provide spaces for witches to exchange ideas, share experiences, and find companionship. These communities can be particularly crucial for solitary practitioners, often offering a virtual coven where members can celebrate Sabbats and Esbats together through synchronized rituals and shared online ceremonies. Here, seasoned practitioners can offer guidance and mentorship to newcomers, which is invaluable in a practice as vast and varied as witchcraft.

Digital Resources for Learning

The wealth of digital resources available today has made learning witchcraft more accessible than ever before. From blogs that offer tutorials on spellcasting to online courses that cover the history and ethics of witchcraft, these resources can be incredible tools for both beginners and experienced practitioners looking to expand their knowledge. Websites like Sacred Texts archive a vast collection of historical occult texts, while platforms like YouTube host countless videos that teach everything from tarot reading to herbal magic. For those who prefer a more structured approach, online schools of witchcraft offer courses complete with certifications. These resources make it possible for anyone with internet access to learn and practice witchcraft, regardless of their location or background.

Ethical Considerations Online

As we embrace the digital integration of witchcraft, we must also consider the ethical implications that come with it. Privacy is a major concern, especially when sharing spells or conducting rituals online. It's important to be mindful of what personal information you share in digital witchcraft spaces and to respect the privacy of others in the community. Additionally, the issue of digital footprints comes into play when sharing spellwork or ritual details online. Once something is shared on the internet, it can be difficult to control where it goes or how it's used. This calls for a cautious approach to what we choose to share and how we share it. Always ensure that your digital practice respects the principles of consent and confidentiality, safeguarding both your own privacy and that of others in your community.

In this digital age, the ancient art of witchcraft is finding new expressions and reaching more people than ever before. Through thoughtful integration of technology, participation in online communities, leveraging digital resources for learning, and adhering to ethical practices online, modern witches are shaping a future where the craft not only survives but thrives. Whether you are a solitary practitioner looking for connection or a seasoned witch seeking to expand your knowledge, the digital world offers a multitude of tools and opportunities to deepen your practice and connect with the global witchcraft community.

1.4 CRAFTING YOUR PERSONAL WITCHCRAFT PRACTICE

Personalizing Your Path

Every witch walks a unique path. Tailoring your witchcraft practice to align with your personal beliefs, lifestyle, and spiritual inclinations is not just beneficial; it's necessary for creating a practice that resonates deeply and sustains your spiritual growth. Begin by reflecting on what drew you to witchcraft. Was it a desire for empowerment, a search for a deeper connection to the natural world, or perhaps a need for personal healing? Your motivations can guide the development of your practice, influencing everything from the deities you choose to work with to the spells you cast.

Consider also your daily responsibilities and lifestyle. If you're a busy professional with limited free time, spells that require lengthy preparations may not be suitable. Instead, focus on crafting shorter rituals or incorporating small, magical acts into your daily routine. Likewise, if you are a parent, involving your children in your practice through simple and safe rituals can be incredibly fulfilling. Remember, there is no single way to be a witch. Whether you live in a bustling city apartment or a quiet rural home, your practice should feel like a natural extension of your life.

For those beginning to shape their path, start small. Choose one or two practices that intrigue you, such as candle magic or herbalism, and dive deep into these areas. Over time, as you grow more confident and your interests expand, your practice will naturally evolve. This evolution is a beautiful part of your witchcraft journey—as you change and grow, so too will your practice. Let it shift and change with you, reflecting who you are at each stage of your life.

Incorporating Daily Routines

Magic doesn't have to be limited to elaborate rituals performed during lunar events. You can weave magic into your daily routines, turning the commonplace into the meaningful. Start your day with a simple grounding exercise, such as visualizing roots growing from your feet deep into the Earth while you brush your teeth or shower. This act doesn't just connect you to the Earth; it also sets a stable, grounded tone for the day ahead.

Meal preparation is another excellent opportunity for incorporating magic into your daily life. As you cook, focus on imbuing your food with specific energies. Chopping carrots? Visualize slicing away obstacles. Stirring a pot? Stir in positivity and peace. Each action can be a spell in itself, transforming your meals into vessels of magical intent. Additionally, consider the magical properties of the ingredients you use. Incorporating herbs with specific correspondences in your cooking not only enhances the flavor but also brings those energies into your life in a very literal way.

Cleaning your home can also be a magical ritual. Create a simple floor wash with vinegar, water, and essential oils like lavender for calmness or peppermint for energy. As you clean, visualize washing away negativity and inviting positive energy into your home. This turns a routine chore into a powerful cleansing ritual, aligning your living space with your spiritual desires.

Setting Intentions

The power of intention is at the heart of effective witchcraft. Setting clear, focused intentions is crucial for directing your magical energies toward the desired outcomes. An intention should be specific, positive, and stated in the present tense as though it is already true. For example, instead of saying, "I don't want to be stressed," frame it positively: "I am calm and centered." This clarity helps to direct your subconscious mind and the energies you are working with toward manifesting your actual desires.

When setting intentions, it's helpful to write them down. This act not only clarifies your thoughts but also solidifies your commitment to them. Place your written intentions on your altar, in a journal, or somewhere you will see them regularly. Revisit them daily through meditation or affirmation practices, reinforcing the energy directed toward your goals. Over time, you will find that the clarity of your intentions directly influences the effectiveness of your magical work, bringing your desires into reality with greater precision and power.

Creating a Personal Altar

Your altar is a sacred space, a physical representation of your spiritual practice, and a focal point for your magical work. Creating a personal altar involves more than just choosing items that resonate with you; it's about creating a reflection of your inner self and your intentions. Start by choosing a space that feels right—whether it's a small corner of a room, a shelf, or an entire table. This space should feel peaceful and powerful to you.

When selecting items for your altar, choose those that have personal significance or magical properties aligned with your intentions. This could include candles, crystals, images of deities or spiritual figures, and elements from nature such as shells, stones, or plants. Each item should serve a purpose, whether it's to attract certain energies, aid in focus, or serve as a tool in your rituals.

Consider also the addition of seasonal elements to

connect your practice to the rhythm of the natural world. For example, fresh flowers in the spring, leaves in the autumn, snow or pinecones in the winter, and sand or seashells in the summer can all serve to align your altar with the energies of the seasons. As you change and grow, your altar should evolve with you, reflecting your current needs, intentions, and spiritual journey.

By creating a personalized practice, incorporating magic into your daily routines, setting clear intentions, and crafting a personal altar, you build a witchcraft practice that not only suits your unique path but also deeply enriches your life. This personalized approach ensures that your practice remains vibrant, relevant, and deeply connected to who you are, allowing you to live magically every day.

1.5 UNDERSTANDING THE POWER OF INTENTION

The concept of intention is foundational in the realm of witchcraft, acting as the steering wheel that guides the energies of our spells and rituals toward specific destinations. Intention in spellwork is much more than just a wish or a hope; it is a clear, focused visualization of the outcome you desire, charged with your willpower and emotional energy. This clarity of purpose is what transforms simple actions into powerful magical practices. For instance, when lighting a candle, one might simply see the act of igniting a wick, but with intention, this ordinary act becomes a beacon calling forth light, warmth, and energy into your life. The key is to define your intentions with precision and imbue them with your personal energies.

It is essential to cultivate a state of clarity and concentration in order to focus your will effectively. Begin by finding a quiet space where you can sit comfortably without interruptions. Close your eyes, take deep, slow breaths, and allow your body to relax. As you ease into a calm state, start to visualize your goal. Imagine it in as much detail as possible—what does achieving this goal look like? How will it feel? Who is involved? Painting a vivid mental picture will help solidify your intention, making it a potent catalyst for your spellwork. This practice not only enhances the effectiveness of your rituals but also aligns your subconscious mind with your conscious goals, creating a powerful coherence that propels you toward your desired outcome.

Visualization techniques are invaluable tools in manifesting these intentions. They allow you to create a mental blueprint of what you wish to achieve, which informs the energy you channel during your magical practices. A useful technique is the visualization of energy flow. Picture your intention as a ball of light, growing brighter and stronger with each breath you take. Visualize this light moving through your body, through your arms, and into the spell or object you are working with, infusing it with your purpose and power. This method not only helps you focus your energies but also connects you deeply with the task at hand, enhancing the personal significance and effectiveness of your ritual.

The balance between intention and ritual is a delicate dance that often leans heavily on intention. While rituals involve specific actions, tools, and words, they are merely vessels for the intentions they carry. A simple spell with a well-crafted, potent intention can be far more effective than the most elaborate ritual lacking a clear purpose. It's crucial, therefore, to spend more time honing your intentions than fussing over the complexities of your ritual setups. This focus shifts your practice from being merely performative to deeply transformative. For example, while a ritual to attract love might involve an array of candles, herbs, and symbols, the core of its power lies in the intention—to open your heart and life to the experience of love, which is clear, focused, and charged with your personal desire and emotional energy.

In practice, this means that whether you are crafting a spell to find a new job, heal from a past hurt, or protect your home, the clarity and strength of your intention are what will determine the success of your spell. It is the heart and soul of your magical practice, the secret ingredient that weaves together your desires with the fabric of reality.

1.6 NAVIGATING CULTURAL SENSITIVITY IN WITCHCRAFT

Understanding the cultural backgrounds of various witchcraft practices not only enriches your own practice but also deepens your respect for the diversity that exists within this spiritual realm. Witchcraft, in its many forms, has been practiced across the globe for centuries, deeply rooted in the traditions and histories of countless cultures. Each of these practices brings a unique perspective and wisdom to the craft, offering us a richer, more nuanced understanding of magic and spirituality. For instance, consider the sacred use of sage in Native American rituals, the intricate Celtic knotwork often used in spellcraft, or the vibrant festivals of West African Vodun. Each tradition provides a window into the soul of the culture from which it originates, and by seeking to understand these backgrounds, we honor the depth and breadth of witchcraft as a global spiritual practice.

When engaging with practices that are not part of your own heritage, it's crucial to approach them with respect and humility. Begin by educating yourself about the cultural, historical, and religious significance of the practices you wish to adopt. This involves more than a quick internet search—it means investing time in reading books, listening to voices from within those cultures, and, if possible, engaging with practitioners who are representatives of the tradition. For example, if you are drawn to the use of crystals commonly employed in Hindu rituals, take the time to learn about the religious and cultural significance of these stones within Hinduism and seek guidance from those who have been raised within this tradition.

Avoiding cultural appropriation is a critical aspect of practicing witchcraft ethically. Appropriation involves taking elements from a culture not your own and using them outside of their original context—often without understanding or respect for their true meaning. This can be harmful, as it reduces profound and sacred practices to mere aesthetics or commodities. To avoid this, always ask yourself whether your use of these elements respects their original meaning and context. Are you contributing to the commodification of a culture, or are you honoring and supporting it? Ensure that your practices do not strip away the significance of sacred symbols and rituals. Instead, focus on learning and honoring the traditions as they are meant to be understood and practiced. When in doubt, the best course of action is to seek out authentic sources or guides who can provide the proper context and understanding needed to engage with these practices respectfully.

Creating an inclusive witchcraft practice means welcoming diversity and learning from others. It involves recognizing that no single tradition holds all the answers and that there is immense value in the varied ways witchcraft is practiced around the world. This inclusivity not only enriches your own practice but also fosters a sense of global community among practitioners of the craft. Celebrate the diversity of witchcraft by participating in events and forums that bring together practitioners from different backgrounds. Engage in exchanges that allow for the sharing of practices, stories, and wisdom across cultural lines. Such interactions can be profoundly enriching, as they allow everyone involved to expand their understanding and appreciation of witchcraft in its many forms.

~

By EMBRACING cultural sensitivity in your witchcraft practice, you contribute to a more respectful and enriched global community of witches. You ensure that your practice not only brings personal growth and empowerment but also fosters respect, understanding, and unity among practitioners from all walks of life. In doing so, you help to weave a tapestry of magical practice that honors its richly diverse roots while looking forward to a future where all can share in the wisdom and beauty of the craft. Live this commitment through every spell you cast and every ritual you perform, carrying forward the spirit of respect and inclusivity that forms the heart of truly transformative witchcraft.

CHAPTER 2
TOOLS AND INGREDIENTS FOR MODERN WITCHCRAFT

In the enchanting realm of witchcraft, each tool and ingredient carries its own magic, a unique whisper of power that can transform the ordinary into the extraordinary. As we delve into the world of magical tools, it's important to remember that the most potent spells often stem from the simplest sources. This chapter is dedicated to uncovering the magic that resides within everyday items—those common, often overlooked objects around your home that hold surprising potential for transformation and empowerment. Let's explore how you can turn the mundane into the magical, crafting a toolkit that not only suits your witchcraft needs but also resonates with your personal energy and intentions.

2.1 EVERYDAY ITEMS AS MAGICAL TOOLS

The Magic of the Mundane

Imagine looking around your home and seeing more than just household items; see potential wands, cauldrons, and talismans. This shift in perspective is the first step in transforming your daily environment into a space brimming with magical possibilities. For example, a simple cooking pot can become your cauldron where potions and soups brew with intentions of healing and love. A wooden spoon can serve as a wand, directing your will and energy as you stir your concoctions. Even the mirrors in your home can act as tools for scrying or for spells that promote self-reflection and clarity. By viewing these objects through a magical lens, you begin to see your world as a vibrant tapestry of tools and symbols, each adding a layer of depth and meaning to your craft.

Household Items for Rituals

The accessibility and potency of household items make them excellent choices for rituals and spellcasting. Consider the following examples: Salt, a common kitchen staple, is powerful in protection spells and in casting circles. It can be used to create boundaries that keep away negative energies. Candles, another readily available item, can be used for color magic—white for purity, black for absorption of negativity, red for passion, and green for prosperity. Herbs like rosemary and basil, often found in kitchens, are fantastic for protection and love spells, respectively. Even something as ordinary as a broom can be used to metaphorically sweep away negative energy from your home. By utilizing these items, your practice becomes not only more sustainable but also deeply personal and intertwined with your daily life.

Creating Your Toolkit

Assembling your first magical toolkit with items you already own is not just economical but also a process filled with personal insight and creativity. Start by selecting items that resonate with you; these might be things you are drawn to because of their texture, color, or any emotional connection you might feel. For instance, a favorite scarf might become an altar cloth, a special cup could serve as a chalice, and a family heirloom might take on new life as a representation of ancestry on your altar. As you choose each item, think about its practical and symbolic uses in your practice. This process not only deepens your connection to your tools but also enhances the personal power of your spells and rituals.

Consecrating Your Tools

Consecrating your tools is a crucial step in preparing them for magical use, as it cleanses them of previous energies and aligns them with your current intentions. A simple method to consecrate your items is through the elements. Start by cleansing each item with water—preferably natural, like rainwater or spring water. Then, pass the item through incense smoke (air) and candle flame (fire) to purify it further. Finally, sprinkle a bit of salt over it (Earth) to ground the energy. As you perform these actions, visualize the item being bathed in a glowing light, ready to work in harmony with your intentions. This process not only prepares your tools physically but also connects them to you energetically, making your magical workings more seamless and potent.

Interactive Element: Visualization Exercise for Tool Consecration

Take a moment now to hold a potential magical tool in your hands. Close your eyes and visualize a clear light enveloping both you and the item. See this light cleansing the tool of all previous energies and see it glowing with potential. Affirm its purpose in your practice, whether it's to direct energy, offer protection, or aid in healing. Feel the bond between you and the item strengthen, charged with your personal intentions. This simple visualization not only deepens your relationship with your tool but also enhances its effectiveness in your magical practice.

By reimagining everyday items as tools of magic, you open up a world of possibilities that encourages a more personal, sustainable, and powerful practice. Each object in your toolkit holds the potential to affect real change, both in your personal sphere and in the broader energies that surround you. As you work with these tools, remember that their true magic comes not from their outward appearance but from the intention and energy you imbue them with.

2.2 THE MODERN WITCH'S GUIDE TO HERBOLOGY

Navigating the verdant world of herbology can transform your magical practice, imbuing it with the energies of the

Earth and connecting you deeper to the rhythm of nature. Herbs are not just culinary delights; they are potent carriers of magic, each with unique properties that can enhance spells, rituals, and daily life. Let's explore how common kitchen herbs can be repurposed in your magical workings, the importance of ethical sourcing, clever substitutions for rare herbs, and the best ways to store and maintain their magical potency.

Herbs such as basil, rosemary, and lavender are likely already in your kitchen or garden, and their uses in magic are as varied as they are in cooking. Basil, often associated with love and protection, can be sprinkled around the home to ward off negative energy or used in love spells to attract romance. Rosemary, a powerful cleanser and protector, can be burnt like incense to purify a space from negative influences and promote healing. Lavender, known for its calming properties, works wonderfully in spells aimed at reducing stress, promoting peaceful sleep, or as an enhancer of love and harmony. Mint, with its invigorating scent, can be used in spells for prosperity and abundance. By incorporating these herbs into your spells or keeping them on your altar, you harness their energies and enhance your magical practice.

Ethically sourcing herbs is crucial in maintaining the integrity of your practice and the balance of our ecosystem. It's important to consider where and how your herbs are grown—opting for those that are cultivated sustainably and without harm to the environment. Foraging for herbs can be a deeply rewarding experience that connects you to the land and the spirit of the plants, but it should be done with respect for nature and adherence to local guidelines. Taking only what you need, leaving plenty for wildlife, and never harvesting endangered plant species are principles that should guide your foraging. Supporting local herb shops or community gardens can also be a wonderful way to find ethically sourced herbs while contributing to your community. These shops often offer the added benefit of providing valuable insights into the uses and properties of less common herbs.

Substituting hard-to-find herbs with more accessible ones ensures that your spellwork remains practical and potent. If a spell calls for a rare or out-of-season herb, several common herbs often share similar properties and can be used as effective substitutes. For instance, if you can't find damiana for a love spell, rose petals are a readily available and powerful alternative. Similarly, if white sage is unavailable for cleansing rituals, juniper or cedar can offer potent purifying qualities. Learning about these correspondences not only makes your practice more adaptable but also deepens your understanding of the properties and relationships between different herbs.

Storing and handling herbs properly is key to preserving their magical and medicinal qualities. Herbs should be kept in a cool, dry place away from direct sunlight to maintain their potency. Glass jars with tight-fitting lids are ideal for storage, as they prevent moisture and light from deteriorating the herbs. Labeling each jar with the herb's name and the date of acquisition helps manage your stock and helps you use older herbs first. For herbs used in spells and rituals, consider dedicating a special set of tools for handling them—such as a specific knife for cutting or a wooden bowl for mixing. This not only keeps the energies of your herbs pure but also infuses them with a sense of sacred purpose, enhancing their effectiveness in your magical work.

By integrating herbology into your witchcraft practice, you embrace a tradition as old as witchcraft itself—connecting with the powers of nature through the humble yet profound magic of herbs. Whether used in kitchen witchery, healing spells, or protective charms, herbs bring a touch of nature's mystery into our lives, making our magical practices richer and more resonant with the energies of the natural world.

2.3 CRYSTALS FOR EVERYDAY EMPOWERMENT

Crystals, with their mesmerizing colors and enchanting geometries, are more than just beautiful natural artifacts. Each crystal resonates with unique energies that can harmonize with your personal intentions, amplifying your desires and supporting your spiritual journey. When choosing crystals for personal empowerment, it's essential to rely on your intuition and personal resonance. This means that the process of selecting a crystal is as personal as the crystal's purpose in your life. When you feel a pull towards a particular crystal, it often indicates that the crystal's energies are a match for your current needs or desires.

For instance, you might find yourself inexplicably drawn to rose quartz, known for its soothing properties and connection to heart-centered energy, during times when you seek more self-love or wish to enhance your relationships.

The process of selecting the right crystal can be quite intuitive. Begin by setting a clear intention for what you need guidance or support with, such as confidence, protection, or clarity. As you browse through crystals, either in a store or online, pay attention to which ones catch your eye or cause a notable emotional or physical reaction. These reactions can range from a sense of calm to a spark of excitement or even a tingling sensation in your hands. Trust these instincts—they are your subconscious recognitions of the energies that are most needed in your life at the moment.

Once you have chosen your crystals, it is crucial to cleanse and charge them to enhance their natural energies and align them with your personal vibrations. Cleansing your crystals removes any lingering energies they may have picked up before coming to you. This can be done in several ways, such as holding them under running water, burying them in the Earth overnight, or smudging them with sage or palo santo smoke. Charging them involves infusing them with your energy and intention. This can be achieved by leaving them out under the moonlight during a full moon, placing them in direct sunlight, or meditating with them, visualizing your intentions flowing into the crystal.

Incorporating crystals into your daily life is a beautiful way to continuously align their potent energies with your personal aura. Wearable crystal jewelry like necklaces, bracelets, or earrings not only serves as a constant reminder of your intentions but also keeps the crystal's energy close to your body, enhancing its impact. Alternatively, placing crystals in your living or workspace can help to create a peaceful, harmonized environment. For example, a clear quartz crystal placed near your workspace can aid in clarity and concentration, while amethyst in the bedroom can promote restful sleep and intuitive dreams.

Crystals are also incredibly effective when used with specific intentions in mind. For love and relationships, rose quartz is the stone of choice as it promotes compassion, peace, and unconditional love. For those seeking protection, black tourmaline is renowned for its ability to block negative energies and electromagnetic frequencies. If prosperity is your focus, citrine is celebrated for attracting wealth and abundance. Meanwhile, amethyst is excellent for spiritual growth and healing, providing a calming energy that enhances meditation and spiritual awareness. Each crystal has a unique vibration, so choosing one that aligns with your specific needs can greatly enhance your spiritual practice and daily life.

By understanding how to select, cleanse, charge, and incorporate crystals into your daily routines, you harness the ability to significantly boost your personal empowerment and spiritual growth. Crystals serve not only as physical reminders of your intentions but also as active participants in your spiritual journey, each resonating with energies that support and uplift your personal aspirations.

2.4 DIGITAL GRIMOIRES: CREATING YOUR OWN ONLINE SPELLBOOK

In the ever-evolving practice of modern witchcraft, the adaptation of digital tools has opened up innovative ways to record and refine our magical workings. Consider the digital grimoire, an electronic version of the traditional book of shadows, which not only stores your spells and rituals but also enhances your practice with its accessibility and ease of organization. Imagine having all your magical knowledge, from herb correspondences to moon phase calendars, right at your fingertips, accessible from anywhere in the world. This convenience is particularly appealing for those of us who are always on the move or who prefer to avoid carrying a physical book. Moreover, the search functionalities of digital formats make organizing and retrieving information effortless. No more flipping through pages to find that one spell you wrote down months ago; a simple keyword search can bring it up in seconds.

The organization of a digital grimoire can be a delightful and creative process, especially with the various platforms available today. Blogs, for instance, offer a chronological arrangement of entries, which can be useful for those who enjoy seeing the progression and changes in their craft over time. Platforms like WordPress or Blogger provide user-friendly interfaces that are easy to set up and customize according to your aesthetic preferences. For those who prioritize privacy and security, dedicated apps designed for journaling or note-taking, such as Evernote or Notion, offer robust encryption options to keep your magical secrets safe. These apps also allow for a more flexible organization, letting you create categories, tags, and databases that make structuring your grimoire a straightforward task. Each platform has its own set of tools and benefits, so consider what aspects are most important to your practice—be it the ease of access, the level of customization, or the strength of privacy features—before deciding where to house your digital grimoire.

Speaking of privacy, securing your digital grimoire is paramount, as it not only contains personal reflections and experiences but may also include sensitive information that could be misused if it falls into the wrong hands. Start by using strong, unique passwords for any accounts associated with your grimoire, and consider enabling two-factor authentication for an added layer of security. Be cautious about which cloud services you use to back up your grimoire; opt for those with strong encryption protocols and a good reputation for protecting user data. Regularly updating your software and apps can also protect you from vulnerabilities that could be exploited by hackers. For an extra layer of privacy, some witches choose to encrypt individual files or entries, especially those that contain the most sacred of their workings or personal information.

Incorporating multimedia elements into your digital grimoire not only enriches the content but also makes the practice of updating and referring to your grimoire more engaging. Consider adding photos of your altar setups or spell outcomes to visually document your practice. Audio recordings of chants, guided meditations, or even just reflections spoken aloud can capture the nuances of your voice and intentions, adding a deeply personal touch. Video entries can be especially powerful for recording rituals or spell demonstrations, providing a dynamic way to revisit and learn from your past practices. These multimedia elements can help transform your grimoire from a mere journal into a living archive of your magical journey, full of texture and vibrancy.

By embracing the digital evolution in witchcraft, you open up a world of possibilities for how you record, practice, and reflect on your craft. A digital grimoire is not just a tool for organization—it's a dynamic companion that grows and adapts with you, offering new ways to explore and express your magic. Whether you're a seasoned witch or just starting out, the digital grimoire holds the potential to enhance your practice with its blend of ancient tradition and modern innovation, making it a truly invaluable asset in your magical arsenal.

2.5 THE ART OF CRAFTING SIGILS FOR PERSONAL USE

Sigils are one of the most personal and versatile tools in the witch's arsenal. Essentially, a sigil is a symbolic representation of an intention, desire, or goal that you wish to manifest. Its power lies in its ability to condense complex ideas into a single, charged symbol that acts as a focal point for your magical energy. The process begins with a clear statement of intent—whether you're seeking to attract love, achieve a professional goal, or enhance your spiritual growth. This intention is then transformed into a visual symbol, which serves as a direct conduit to your subconscious, bypassing the more skeptical parts of your mind to work on a deeper, more instinctual level.

Creating a sigil starts with writing down your intention as clearly and succinctly as possible. Focus on being specific; for example, instead of "I want to be happy," you might write, "I attract joy and contentment daily." Once your intention is set, you begin the process of transformation. One common method involves writing out your intention, removing any repeated letters, and then further breaking down the remaining letters into simpler shapes and lines. These elements are then creatively recombined to form a new, abstract symbol that is both unique and meaningful to you. This process not only focuses your intent but also starts to charge the sigil with your personal energy and desire.

Another intriguing method for crafting sigils involves the use of magic squares or kamea, ancient grids associated with various planets that correspond to different energies and intentions. Each letter of your intention is assigned a number, and a continuous line is drawn across the grid connecting these numbers, resulting in a geometric design that holds the essence of your wish. This method can add an additional layer of astrological or elemental correspondence to your sigil, aligning it more closely with the energies of the universe.

Once your sigil is created, activating and charging it is the next crucial step. This activation is essentially an act of empowering the sigil, turning it from a mere drawing into a potent magical tool. This can be done in various ways depending on your personal practice and the nature of the intention. Some may choose to meditate with the sigil, focusing deeply on its meaning while visualizing their goal being achieved. Others might use elements like fire or water to empower it—burning the sigil can release its energy into the universe, while submerging it in water can imbue it with emotional clarity and purity. The method of activation often depends on the nature of the intention and your personal resonance with the elements.

Incorporating sigils into your daily life can be both practical and creative. Sigils can be drawn on the body with henna or washable ink as a form of magical body art—a constant reminder and activator of your intentions. You might also engrave them on jewelry or create amulets that carry your sigils with you throughout the day. Incorporating sigils into home decor is another effective way to maintain the presence of your intentions in your living space. Carve them into candles to be illuminated with specific purposes in mind, or paint them onto stones to be placed around your home or garden. Each placement not only keeps the sigil's energy active but also integrates your magical practice into your everyday environment, making your entire living space a reflection of your magical intentions.

By mastering the art of sigil creation, you harness a powerful tool that personalizes and intensifies your magical practice. Sigils allow you to manifest changes in the world around you by embedding your deepest desires into symbols that resonate with your personal energy, transforming your outer reality from the inside out. As you experiment with different methods and incorporate these symbols into your life, you'll discover just how effective this beautiful, magical art form can be in manifesting your personal goals and intentions.

2.6 ETHICALLY SOURCING YOUR WITCHCRAFT SUPPLIES

In the realm of modern witchcraft, where the energies we engage with are as important as the outcomes we seek, the principle of 'harm none' extends beyond our spells and into the very materials we use. Ethical sourcing of witchcraft supplies is not just about avoiding negative energies but fostering a practice that supports and nourishes the environment and communities we draw from. This commitment to ethical sourcing ensures that our practices contribute positively to the world, reinforcing the cycles of giving and receiving that are central to the natural balance.

The importance of ethically sourcing supplies cannot be overstated. Every item you use carries energy, not just from the material itself but from the process through which it was acquired. When you choose supplies that are harvested respectfully and responsibly, you are embedding your practice with a deeper level of harmony and integrity. For example, when acquiring stones or herbs, considering their origins and the methods used to gather them can greatly influence the energetic quality of your works. Ethically sourced materials are more likely to carry energies of respect and care, which can enhance your magical workings and align them more closely with the natural world.

Identifying ethical sources for your witchcraft supplies involves a bit of research and mindfulness. Begin by asking vendors about the origin of their goods and the methods used in their cultivation or production. Are the crystals you are purchasing conflict-free? Are the herbs organically grown without harming the environment? Questions like these not only inform you about the product but also signal to vendors that there is a demand for ethically sourced materials, which can encourage more sustainable practices industry-wide. Additionally, look for certifications or endorsements from credible organizations that advocate for ethical environmental practices. These can often be a reliable indicator of a vendor's commitment to ethical sourcing.

Supporting local and small businesses within the magical community is a powerful way to practice ethical sourcing. Small businesses, particularly those that specialize in witchcraft supplies, often have a direct relationship with their sourcing and are mindful of their environmental impact. By purchasing from these vendors, not only are you obtaining materials that are more likely to be ethically sourced, but you are also strengthening the economic base of your own community. This support helps sustain a market for ethically sourced goods and encourages other businesses to consider their sourcing practices. Moreover, local businesses are often able to provide the backstory of their items, offering a personal connection and deeper understanding of the supplies you are incorporating into your practice.

Sustainable witchcraft practices extend beyond just where and how we buy our supplies—they encompass how we use and dispose of them as well. To enhance the sustainability of your practice, consider ways to reduce waste and reuse materials. For instance, candle remnants can be melted down and reformed, and herb clippings can be used to make infused oils or added to compost. Embracing practices that reduce your ecological footprint not only aligns with the ethical tenets of modern witchcraft but also deepens your connection to the Earth and its cycles. These practices remind us that we are part of a larger ecosystem and that our spiritual practices can reflect a harmonious balance with the natural world.

By integrating these principles of ethical sourcing and sustainability into your witchcraft, you create a practice that is not only powerful in its magical workings but also profound in its respect and reverence for the natural and human resources it engages with. This approach ensures that your practice 'harms none' and contributes positively to the world, embodying the true spirit of witchcraft.

As we wrap up this exploration of ethically sourcing your witchcraft supplies, remember that the choices you make about where to obtain your materials are as crucial as the spells you cast. Each decision is a stitch in the tapestry of your magical practice, woven with the energies of respect, sustainability, and community support. These choices help shape a practice that not only seeks personal growth and empowerment but also contributes to the well-being of the Earth and its inhabitants.

CONTINUING FORWARD, we turn our attention to the next chapter, where we will delve into the enchanting world of ritual crafting. Here, we will explore how to bring together the tools and ingredients we've discussed, weaving them into rituals that resonate with power and purpose, further enhancing your journey in modern witchcraft.

CHAPTER 3
SPELLS FOR SELF-DISCOVERY AND PERSONAL GROWTH

I magine standing under the vast expanse of the night sky, the moon casting a soft, silvery glow that bathes the world in an ethereal light. This celestial body, a constant presence and ever-changing through its phases, has captivated human imagination and spirituality for centuries. The moon's cyclical journey from new to full mirrors our own paths of growth and renewal. In this chapter, we explore how connecting with the lunar energies can serve as a powerful catalyst for personal transformation and self-discovery. Each phase of the moon offers unique energies that, when harnessed through spellwork, can support your personal development and help manifest your deepest desires.

3.1 MOON PHASES AND PERSONAL GROWTH SPELLS

Connecting with Lunar Energies

The moon's cycle is a metaphor for the cycle of our own lives, encompassing birth, growth, death, and rebirth. Each phase of the moon resonates with different aspects of personal growth and self-discovery. The new moon, with its promise of beginnings, invites us to plant seeds of intention. The waxing moon, a time of growth and accumulation, encourages us to take action towards these intentions. The full moon, bright and complete, is a period for reflection and celebration of progress, while the waning moon supports us in letting go of what no longer serves us, preparing us to start anew. By aligning your personal growth spells with these phases, you harness specific energies that amplify your intentions and facilitate your journey of self-discovery.

New Moon Intentions

The new moon is a blank slate, the perfect time to set intentions for what you wish to bring into your life. Imagine this phase as a fertile ground, ready to nurture the seeds of your goals and aspirations. A spell to set intentions during the new moon might involve writing down your desires on a piece of paper, then planting it in the Earth or a pot of soil as you visualize your intentions growing with the moon's light. You might also light a white candle to symbolize new beginnings, focusing your mind on the flame as you clearly visualize achieving your goals. This simple ritual not only sets the stage for what you wish to attract but also aligns your energy with the expansive potential of the coming lunar cycle.

Full Moon Release

The full moon is a powerful time for releasing what is no longer needed in your life. It's a time to let go of old patterns, negative thoughts, or any obstacles that hinder your personal growth. A ritual during this phase might involve writing down these impediments on paper and then safely burning the paper in a fireproof container as you visualize your obstacles being consumed by the flames. Alternatively, you could gather stones that represent your burdens and throw them into a body of water or bury them, symbolically casting away your limitations. This act of release is cathartic, helping you clear out old energies to make room for new growth and opportunities.

Waxing and Waning Cycles

The waxing phase of the moon, as it grows fuller, supports spells that attract things into your life, be it love, prosperity, or health. A spell in this phase might involve creating a charm bag filled with items that symbolize what you wish to attract, such as coins for prosperity or rose petals for love. Keep this charm bag with you as the moon grows fuller, and visualize your desires manifesting into reality. Conversely, the waning moon helps in banishing negativity or obstacles. During this phase, you might perform a spell that involves sweeping your house with a broom, visualizing sweeping out all negativity and obstacles from your life as the moon decreases in size.

Interactive Element: Journaling Prompt for Lunar Reflection

To deepen your connection with the lunar energies, maintain a moon phase journal. For each phase, jot down how you feel, what challenges you face, and what dreams you have. Reflect on how the moon's energy might be influencing these aspects of your life, and note any patterns that emerge. This practice not only enhances your awareness of the lunar influences but also helps you align more closely with its cycles, making your spellwork even more powerful.

By engaging with the spells and rituals outlined in this section, you tap into the profound energies of the moon, aligning your personal growth with the natural rhythms of the universe. This alignment facilitates a deeper connection with your inner self, empowering you to manifest transformation and discover your true potential through the magical path of lunar witchcraft.

3.2 CREATING SPACE FOR SELF-DISCOVERY THROUGH WITCHCRAFT

Creating a sacred space is akin to crafting a personal sanctuary where you can retreat to explore the depths of your soul, meditate, reflect, and engage in spellwork. This space serves as a physical representation of your commitment to your spiritual journey, enveloping you in an atmosphere that nurtures personal growth and self-discovery. One effective way to establish such a space involves performing a consecration ritual, which not only dedicates the space to your spiritual work but also clears it of any discordant energies. Start by choosing a spot that feels inherently peaceful to you, where interruptions are minimal. This could be a corner of a room, a part of your garden, or anywhere that you can consistently access and feel at ease. Cleanse this chosen area physically by tidying up and removing any clutter, as a clean space promotes a clear mind. Next, smudge the area with sage or sweetgrass, or if smoke is an issue, a spritz of moon water mixed with essential oils like lavender or sandalwood can be just as effective. As you do this, visualize any residual negativity dissipating, leaving behind only serene, welcoming energy. Finally, declare your intention for the space—speak aloud that this is now your sacred space, dedicated to growth, wisdom, and spiritual exploration.

Setting up an altar can further enhance this sacred space, acting as a focal point for your spiritual activities. When constructing an altar dedicated to personal growth, incorporate elements that symbolize transformation and self-reflection. A simple setup might include a small mirror to symbolize self-examination, a feather to represent the freedom to change and adapt, and a series of stones like amethyst for peace, black tourmaline for protection against negative thoughts, and citrine for personal power and the manifestation of your intentions. The colors you choose should soothe or energize you, depending on your needs; soft blues and purples can calm the mind, while vibrant oranges and yellows might stimulate creativity and personal drive. Arrange these items in a way that feels harmonious and meaningful to you. This altar is a personal touchstone, a place to come back to time and again to center yourself and focus on your personal evolution.

Cleansing your space regularly is crucial in maintaining clarity and openness to insights. Energetic clutter can accumulate just as physical clutter does, and it can obscure your spiritual vision, making it harder to connect with your deeper self. Besides regular smudging or spraying with moon water, consider incorporating sound cleansing into your routine. Ringing a bell with a clear tone or playing a singing bowl can help break up stagnant energy in the space. Do this at least once a week or more often if the space feels heavy or if you've been doing a lot of intense emotional or spiritual work there. This maintenance not only keeps the space feeling fresh and vibrant but also reaffirms your commitment to keeping your spiritual pathway clear.

Connecting with nature offers another profound way to enhance your personal growth practices. Nature inherently possesses powerful energies that can help you connect more deeply with your inner self and the universe. If possible, establish an outdoor sacred space, perhaps in a garden, by a body of water, or in a secluded spot in a local park. Bring elements of nature into your indoor space if an outdoor setup isn't feasible; houseplants, natural objects like shells or stones, or even a small fountain can help bring the essence of nature indoors. When practicing in these natural settings, be mindful of your impact on the environment—use biodegradable materials, do not take more from the land than what you need for your practice, and always leave the space as clean as or cleaner than you found it. This respect ensures that the energies you work with are pure and that your spiritual practice is sustainable and harmonious with the Earth's rhythms.

By creating and maintaining a sacred space, setting up a personal altar, regularly cleansing your spiritual environment, and incorporating elements of nature, you build a strong foundation for profound self-discovery and personal growth. These practices not only deepen your connection to your inner self but also align you more closely with the energies of the universe, facilitating a journey of continuous transformation and enlightenment.

3.3 ENHANCING YOUR INTUITION WITH SPELLCRAFT

Intuition is like a quiet voice within you, guiding you through the unseen realms of your subconscious wisdom. It's a natural, yet often underutilized, tool that can significantly enhance your decision-making, creativity, and connection to the spiritual world. To strengthen this innate ability through witchcraft, consider incorporating intuition-boosting spells that utilize everyday items. For instance, a simple yet effective spell involves using a bay leaf, a symbol of wisdom and clarity. Write a single word that represents what you seek clarity on, such as "decisions" or "path," on the leaf. Place it under your pillow before you sleep, or burn it as you meditate, focusing on clearing mental clutter and enhancing your inner knowing.

As the bay leaf transforms either through your dreams or through the smoke, envision your mind opening wider, making room for insights and intuitions to flow freely. This act, simple in execution, can powerfully align your subconscious with your conscious, bringing forth a clearer understanding of the messages your intuition tries to convey.

Dreamwork is another profound method for tapping into your intuitive wisdom. Our dreams are direct communications from our subconscious, providing insights that our waking minds might overlook or suppress. To harness guidance from your dreams, create a dream intention sachet—a small bag filled with herbs like mugwort and lavender, known for their dream-enhancing qualities. Place this sachet under your pillow to stimulate vivid, insightful dreams. Before you sleep, set a clear intention to receive guidance through your dreams, focusing on a particular question or area of your life. Keep a dream journal beside your bed, and upon waking, immediately record any dreams or feelings experienced during the night. Over time, patterns or symbols may emerge that offer clarity or solutions to your waking life queries. This practice not only strengthens your intuition but also deepens your connection to the subconscious mind, revealing the profound wisdom you hold within.

Meditative practices are essential tools for nurturing your intuition. Meditation clears the mental chatter that often clouds our intuitive insights, creating a quiet space for them to surface. Begin with mindful breathing exercises, focusing solely on your breath to help anchor your mind in the present moment. This practice reduces stress and centers your mind, making it more receptive to intuitive hits. Once you've achieved a state of calm, visualize a third eye on your forehead—the seat of intuition in many spiritual traditions. Imagine this eye opening slowly, expanding your ability to see beyond the physical. You can enhance this meditation by holding or placing a crystal known for its intuition-boosting properties, such as lapis lazuli or sodalite, on your forehead. These stones are believed to stimulate the third eye chakra, enhancing psychic abilities and deepening your meditative experience. By regularly engaging in these meditative practices, you nurture a strong, responsive intuition that can guide you in your daily life and spiritual practices.

Lastly, integrating specific crystals and herbs into your daily life can serve as continuous support for your intuitive development. Crystals like amethyst and moonstone are celebrated for their ability to enhance psychic abilities and intuition. Place these crystals around your home, carry them with you, or wear them as jewelry to keep their intuitive energies close. Herbs such as rosemary and juniper can be used in teas or as incense to stimulate mental clarity and psychic powers. Create a small altar or dedicated space in your home where you can regularly interact with these items, setting intentions to strengthen your intuition each time you pass by or pause at this sacred spot. This constant physical reminder of your intention helps to keep your subconscious mind focused on developing your intuitive abilities, making them more accessible in your conscious state.

By weaving these practices into your witchcraft, you create a powerful synergy that continuously nurtures and enhances your intuition. Whether through simple spells, dream work, meditation, or the strategic use of crystals and herbs, you are equipped to unlock the full potential of your inner wisdom, guiding you more effectively through your magical practices and everyday life.

3.4 THE POWER OF SOLITARY RITUALS FOR EMPOWERMENT

In the quiet moments of solitude, where the world's noise fades into the background, lies a profound opportunity for personal empowerment and magical exploration. Designing personal rituals that are uniquely yours, tailored to your individual needs and aspirations, is not just an act of self-care—it's a declaration of your autonomy in your spiritual practice. When you create a ritual from your own experiences and desires, it resonates deeply, becoming a powerful tool for personal transformation. Begin by identifying what empowerment means to you. Is it about gaining confidence, finding peace, or perhaps cultivating strength? Once your goal is clear, consider what symbols, actions, and items represent these concepts to you. For example, if you seek to cultivate inner peace, you might design a ritual that includes elements like water for its calming properties, blue candles for tranquility, and lavender for relaxation. The ritual could involve a bath where you allow the soothing properties of water and lavender to wash away your stress, accompanied by a soft blue candlelight to enhance the calming atmosphere. By personalizing your ritual in this manner, you connect more deeply with its purpose, enhancing its effectiveness and making your practice a true reflection of your innermost needs.

Solitary full moon rituals are particularly potent for self-empowerment and realization. Under the luminous glow of the full moon, you can tap into the heightened energies and the symbolic illumination it provides. One such ritual might involve standing under the moonlight, preferably in a quiet outdoor space where you can see the moon, and performing a simple release and empower practice. Begin by writing down the traits or habits you wish to release on small pieces of paper—things that no longer serve your higher self. One by one, safely burn these papers in a fire-safe bowl, visualizing each limitation being transformed by the fire into new opportunities. Following this, affirm your strengths and aspirations aloud, declaring your intentions to the moon and to yourself. This act of vocal affirmation under the full moon's watchful eye can be incredibly powerful, reinforcing your personal commitment to growth and empowerment.

Incorporating daily empowerment practices into your routine ensures that your connection to your magical practice is active and evolving. These rituals need not be elaborate; even the simplest acts can be woven with intention to significantly empower your day. Each morning, consider starting with a simple candle meditation. Choose a candle color that corresponds to your daily intention—red for vitality, yellow for confidence, or green for growth. As you light the candle, focus on igniting those qualities within you. Spend a few minutes watching the flame, envisioning it fueling your inner strengths with each flicker and glow. This daily ritual, taking just a few moments, sets a tone of empowerment and purpose for your day ahead, continuously nurturing your personal growth.

Finally, embracing solitude as a strength in your witchcraft practice can lead to profound depths of self-discovery and empowerment. Solitary practice forces you to rely on your intuition, to listen deeply to your inner voice, and to trust in your unique magical abilities. It allows you the space to experiment, to learn from your successes and your mistakes, and to truly hone your craft without outside influences. Use this time to explore aspects of magic and spirituality that particularly resonate with you, whether that's spell crafting, divination, herbal magic, or any other area. The insights and growth that come from such deep, personal exploration are often powerful and transformative, fostering a sense of self-reliance and confidence in your abilities as a practitioner. This empowerment, born from the quiet moments spent alone with your craft, not only enhances your magical practices but also permeates other areas of your life, imbuing them with a sense of confidence and self-assuredness that is truly magical.

3.5 SPELLCASTING FOR OVERCOMING PERSONAL BLOCKAGES

In the tapestry of life, each of us may occasionally find threads that seem tangled or knots that are particularly tight; these are the personal blockages that can hinder our growth and prevent us from moving forward. Recognizing and addressing these blockages is a crucial step in personal development. Often, these obstacles are not external but internal, manifesting as fears, old wounds, or limiting beliefs that we have unconsciously held onto. Identifying these can be a process of introspection—looking inward through meditation or reflective practices where you ask yourself what fears or memories are holding you back. A helpful method is to write down your thoughts and feelings regularly. Over time, patterns may emerge from these entries, highlighting recurring fears or anxieties that could be forming blockages. Understanding the root cause of these emotional barriers is the first step in addressing them through spellwork.

Once you've identified these personal blockages, spell-casting can serve as a powerful tool to help clear these obstacles and pave the way for a smoother path forward. A simple but effective spell involves crafting a barrier-breaking oil, which can be used to anoint candles or your-self before undertaking tasks that challenge your blockages. To create this oil, blend basil oil for removal of obstacles, rosemary oil for mental clarity, and a few drops of lemon oil for purification. As you mix these oils, focus on your intention to clear the path ahead of you. Use this oil to anoint a candle, ideally orange for its association with success and overcoming challenges, and light the candle as you visualize the obstacles melting away with the wax.

Another powerful aspect of spellwork for overcoming blockages is the incorporation of rituals that imbue you with courage and strength. These qualities are essential when facing deep-seated fears or making significant changes that your blockages have hindered. A ritual to consider involves the element of water, known for its purifying and renewing properties. Begin by drawing a bath and adding sea salt for purification, chamomile for peace, and tiger's eye stones for courage. As you soak, envision the water imbuing you with the strength and bravery needed to overcome your obstacles. Think of the bath as a rebirth, washing away the old fears and emerging renewed with vigor and fortitude.

In conjunction with these spells and rituals, the use of affirmations and visualizations can significantly amplify your efforts to remove blockages. Affirmations are positive, empowering statements that, when repeated frequently, can help reprogram your subconscious mind, replacing negative thoughts and patterns with positive ones. Create a set of affirmations that directly address your blockages, such as "I release fear and welcome growth" or "I am capable and strong." Integrate these affirmations into your daily routine, repeating them each morning, or write them on pieces of paper that you keep with you throughout the day. Visualization, on the other hand, involves picturing yourself successfully overcoming your blockages. Spend a few minutes each day closing your eyes and imagining a scene where you face a fear or challenge and overcome it triumphantly. This mental practice not only prepares you for the actual event but also builds neural pathways that enhance your ability to act when the situation arises in reality.

By integrating these practices—identifying blockages, utilizing spellwork, engaging in empowering rituals, and reinforcing efforts with affirmations and visualizations— you create a robust framework for personal development. This approach not only aids in overcoming existing blockages but also fortifies you against potential future obstacles, enabling a journey of continuous growth and self-improvement. As you regularly engage in these practices, you'll find that what once seemed like insurmountable blockages begin to dissolve, clearing the way for new opportunities and a deeper understanding of your personal power and potential.

3.6 INCORPORATING ANCESTRAL WISDOM IN MODERN SPELLS

The threads that connect us to our ancestors are woven with wisdom, strength, and experiences that transcend time. Tapping into this rich heritage can profoundly deepen your magical practice, offering guidance and insights that have been refined through generations. The process of connecting with your ancestors in a respectful and safe manner begins with establishing a clear intention to engage with their wisdom to enhance your personal growth. This connection is not about summoning spirits in a trivial manner but about honoring and learning from the lives they led and the knowledge they accumulated. (Read more about Ancestral Witchcraft in Volume III of The Witch Within.)

Creating a space dedicated to your ancestors is a powerful way to start this connection. This can be an ancestral altar, a sacred area in your home where you can communicate with and honor your ancestors. Setting up this altar involves selecting items that represent or were connected to your ancestors. These might include photographs, heirlooms, or even simple objects such as a piece of jewelry or a book. Additionally, include elements that symbolize the four elements—Earth, air, fire, and water—as these are fundamental to many spiritual practices and can help in grounding the energy of the space. Earth can be represented by stones or soil, air by incense, fire by candles, and water by a small bowl of water. As you arrange these items, focus on your intentions, asking for guidance and protection from your ancestral line. This altar becomes a focal point for your interactions with your ancestors, a place where you can offer thanks, seek wisdom, and celebrate their lives.

Integrating the stories and lessons from your ancestors into your spells and rituals can significantly enhance their effectiveness and deepen your personal growth. Each story or lesson handed down through generations carries with it energies of resilience, wisdom, and experience. For instance, you might have been told stories about an ancestor's courage during difficult times or their wisdom in handling complex family dynamics. Reflect on these stories and draw parallels to your own life challenges. Use these reflections in your spellwork by creating spells that invoke the same qualities that helped your ancestors. For example, if an ancestor was known for their healing abilities, you might craft a healing spell that incorporates their favorite herbs or tools, invoking their spirit to guide and enhance your healing work.

Engaging in rituals to seek blessings and guidance from your ancestors can be particularly empowering. One powerful ritual involves writing letters to your ancestors, expressing your current challenges, and asking for their guidance or blessings. Place these letters on your ancestral altar and light a candle to symbolize your request being received. Alternatively, you might hold a small feast at your altar, offering foods that your ancestors enjoyed or that are traditional to your cultural background. As you eat, share stories of your ancestors or simply reflect on their lives, asking them to join you and bless your endeavors. These acts of connection not only honor your ancestors but also weave their enduring presence and wisdom into your life's fabric, empowering you to face challenges with their strength and guidance.

By incorporating these practices into your witchcraft, you create a bridge between the past and the present, allowing the ancestral wisdom to flow into your modern spells and enrich your spiritual journey. This connection not only enhances your personal growth but also pays homage to those who came before you, ensuring their stories and wisdom continue to influence and guide future generations. As you move through your magical practice, remember that you are supported not just by your immediate surroundings but also by the vast network of your ancestors, whose experiences and wisdom pulse through your veins, ready to be tapped for guidance, strength, and protection.

~

As we close this section on incorporating ancestral wisdom into modern spells, we reflect on the profound connections and deep roots that enhance our magical practices and personal growth. Tapping into the wisdom of our ancestors provides not only guidance and strength but also a sense of belonging and continuity that enriches our spiritual journey. As we turn to the next chapter, we carry forward the lessons and blessings of our forebears, ready to apply them to our continuing exploration of the magical arts.

CHAPTER 4
LOVE AND RELATIONSHIPS IN MODERN WITCHCRAFT

In the radiant weave of life, the threads of love and relationships form a vibrant part of the tapestry. Here in this chapter, we explore the magic that resides not just in external connections but begins within the sacred self. The journey to external love often mirrors the pathways we forge within our own hearts. As you delve into these magical practices, remember that the most profound relationship you will ever cultivate is the one with yourself. It's from this inner sanctuary of self-love and acceptance that all other forms of love flow—effortlessly and abundantly.

4.1 SELF-LOVE SPELLS FOR EMPOWERMENT

Crafting Self-Love Spells

The art of crafting self-love spells is a gentle yet

powerful way to affirm your worth and nurture your soul. These spells are your secret garden, a place where you plant the seeds of self-acceptance and watch them bloom into a lush landscape of self-esteem and love. Consider a simple candle spell to ignite the flame of self-love within you. Choose a pink candle, the color of gentle love, and anoint it with rose oil, symbolizing love and harmony. As you dress the candle, visualize your love for yourself growing, enveloping you in a warm, nurturing light. Light the candle and say, "I am love, I am light, self-love is my right." Let the candle burn down, releasing your intention into the universe. This simple spell acts as a beacon, calling back to you the love that you pour out into the world.

Daily Self-Love Rituals

Integrating self-love into your daily rituals can transform tired routines into acts of kindness towards yourself, reinforcing feelings of worth and beauty each day. Begin each morning by standing in front of a mirror, looking into your own eyes, and offering yourself a compliment or words of encouragement, just as you would to a dear friend. This practice, though simple, can profoundly shift your self-perception over time, gradually replacing self-criticism with compassion and appreciation. Another nurturing daily ritual involves creating a self-love tea blend. Use herbs like rose petals for loving energy, jasmine for its uplifting properties, and chamomile for calm. As you sip this tea, imagine drinking in self-love and exhaling any self-doubt or negativity.

Crystals and Herbs for Self-Love

Incorporating crystals and herbs into your self-love spells and rituals can amplify your intentions, embedding them with the earth's nurturing energies. Rose quartz is the stone of unconditional love and is particularly potent in fostering self-love. Keep a piece of rose quartz on your bedside table or wear it as jewelry to remind yourself of your inherent worth. Rhodonite is another powerful crystal for self-love, promoting forgiveness and self-acceptance. Pair these crystals with herbs like lavender for calming, basil for harmony, and cinnamon for warming the heart. Create a self-love sachet with these ingredients and carry it with you, or place it under your pillow to enhance feelings of self-love as you sleep.

Affirmations for Self-Love

Affirmations are powerful tools for reinforcing the magic of self-love in your daily life. They work by slowly reshaping your subconscious patterns of thought, replacing negative self-talk with positive, affirming statements. Start by writing down affirmations that resonate with your personal needs, such as "I deeply and completely love and accept myself" or "I am worthy of all the goodness life offers." Repeat these affirmations each morning or anytime you need a boost of self-love. Write them on sticky notes and place them around your home or workspace as constant reminders of your worth. Engaging with these affirmations regularly not only uplifts your spirits but also strengthens the effectiveness of your self-love spells, weaving a stronger spell of self-acceptance and love around your daily life.

Interactive Element: Journaling Prompt for Self-Love Reflection

Take a moment to reflect on your journey with self-love. Grab your journal and write about the moments when you felt truly at peace with who you are. What were you doing? Who were you with? Use these insights to create more moments like these and plan one small action you can take this week to show yourself love. This reflective practice can help identify what truly makes you feel loved and appreciated by yourself, guiding your continued practice of self-love.

By embracing these spells, rituals, and practices, you create a nurturing foundation of self-love that not only transforms your relationship with yourself but also sets the stage for healthier and more fulfilling relationships with others. As you cultivate this inner sanctuary of love, watch as it overflows, enhancing every connection you make, rooted in the profound truth that love, indeed, starts within.

4.2 ATTRACTING POSITIVE RELATIONSHIPS WITH SPELLCRAFT

Ethical Attraction Spells

The essence of ethical attraction spells lies in their intention to draw positive, nourishing relationships into your life without manipulating the will or emotions of others. These spells encourage the universe to bring you closer to individuals who will naturally resonate with your spirit and enrich your life. A foundational ethical attraction spell might involve creating an attraction sachet filled with natural elements that symbolize love and connection. Ingredients might include pink rose petals for romantic love, cinnamon for warmth and attraction, and orris root for deepening bonds. As you assemble this sachet, focus your intentions on attracting relationships that will bring mutual growth and joy. Seal the sachet and keep it in your home, or carry it with you, visualizing how each day brings you closer to finding meaningful connections. This practice not only sets the stage for new relationships but also aligns your energy with the type of connections you wish to culti-vate, ensuring they are rooted in authenticity and mutual respect.

Friendship Strengthening Spells

Friendships are the bedrock of our social lives, providing support, joy, and companionship. To strengthen these bonds or to attract new like-minded friends, consider a spell that nurtures existing relationships and opens the door to new ones. One effective ritual involves the use of a friendship candle—choose a color that represents friend-ship to you, such as yellow for shared joy or green for growth together. Carve the names of your current friends and traits you value in friends into the candle. As the candle burns, meditate on your appreciation for your friends and visualize your circle widening to include new faces. This spell not only honors the friends you have but also sets the intention to attract more fulfilling friendships into your life, enriching your social circle with genuine connections.

Enhancing Relationship Compatibility

Even the strongest relationships can benefit from spells that enhance compatibility and understanding. For couples looking to deepen their connection, a compatibility spell can realign energies to promote greater harmony and understanding. Begin by creating two charm bags—one for you and one for your partner. Fill each bag with herbs that represent your individual strengths and shared desires, such as basil for harmony, lavender for peace, and rose quartz for loving energy. Exchange bags with your partner, each keeping the other's bag to hold or keep in a personal space. This exchange symbolizes a mutual acceptance and appreciation of each other's individuality and shared path, reinforcing the bond and promoting a deeper under-standing of each other's needs and dreams.

Rituals for Openness and Vulnerability

Openness and vulnerability are critical ingredients in healthy relationships, allowing for a deeper connection and emotional intimacy. Crafting a ritual to enhance these qualities can transform the way you relate to others, making your interactions more genuine and heart-centered. A simple yet profound ritual involves a shared bath with your partner or a close friend, using waters infused with herbs like chamomile for calm and honesty and honey for sweetness and openness. As you both soak, take turns sharing something personal or a feeling you've been holding back. This shared experience not only fosters a deeper emotional connection but also creates a sacred space for honesty and vulnerability within your relationship. This ritual can be particularly transformative, breaking down walls and deepening the trust and connection between you and your loved ones.

By engaging in these practices, you consciously weave magic into your relationships, attracting and nurturing connections that are deeply rooted in mutual respect, understanding, and genuine affection. As you continue to explore these spells and rituals, remember that the most enduring relationships are built on a foundation of honesty, respect, and a genuine desire for mutual growth. Whether you are seeking to strengthen friendships, enhance compatibility, or foster openness and vulnerability, these magical practices offer a pathway to richer, more fulfilling relationships.

4.3 HEALING FROM HEARTBREAK WITH WITCHCRAFT

Navigating through the delicate aftermath of heartbreak or loss, you might find yourself seeking solace and healing that transcends conventional remedies. Witchcraft offers a profound way to address the emotional wounds left by such experiences, facilitating a journey toward healing and renewal. Among the most potent tools at your disposal are spells specifically designed to mend a broken heart. These spells do not erase memories but rather help you to heal from the pain, allowing you to move forward with strength and clarity. A healing spell might involve writing down your feelings of hurt and betrayal on a piece of natural paper and then carefully burning the paper in a fire-safe bowl. As the paper burns, visualize the flames consuming your pain, transforming it into ash that will nourish the growth of new experiences. This ritual allows you to let go of the hurt while affirming your resilience and capacity to heal.

Enhancing this process, consider incorporating a cord-cutting ritual, which is particularly effective for severing emotional ties that bind you to past relationships. This ritual acknowledges that while relationships may end, the energetic cords formed during these connections can linger, continuing to influence your emotional health. To perform a cord-cutting ritual, you will need a black candle for banishing the old, a white candle for new beginnings, and a piece of string to represent the ties you wish to sever. Begin by anointing both candles with an oil infused with healing herbs such as rosemary or eucalyptus. Light the black candle and visualize the negative aspects of the relationship. Then, take the string and, while focusing on your desire to release the past, cut it through with a ceremonial knife or scissors. Finally, light the white candle and focus on your journey toward healing and the new opportunities that await you. This powerful ritual acts as a declaration of independence from past hurts, reinforcing your emotional boundaries and paving the way for new, healthier relationships.

Water, with its intrinsic cleansing properties, is a natural ally in rituals designed to wash away sorrow and pain. A bath ritual for emotional cleansing not only soothes the spirit but also facilitates the release of lingering sadness or bitterness. Prepare a healing bath by infusing the water with sea salt for purification and adding healing herbs such as lavender for tranquility and chamomile for emotional soothing. As you sink into the water, allow yourself to feel the weight of your grief and heartache. Envision the water absorbing your pain, washing it away as you slowly breathe out. You can also softly speak affirmations of healing and renewal or play calming music to enhance the ritual's therapeutic effects. When you emerge from the bath, imagine stepping out renewed, leaving the remnants of past hurts behind in the water, ready to be drained away.

To further support your emotional healing, integrating specific crystals and herbs into your spells and rituals can offer additional comfort and strength. Crystals such as rose quartz and malachite are particularly beneficial for heart healing. Rose quartz promotes self-love and emotional healing, helping to soothe heartache, while malachite is known for its ability to draw out deep-seated feelings and facilitate emotional processing. You can carry these crystals with you, place them under your pillow while you sleep, or hold them during meditation. Pairing these crystals with herbs like hawthorn, which is renowned for its heart-healing properties, and yarrow, which protects against negative energies, can enhance the healing process. Create a small sachet of these herbs and crystals to keep by your bedside or in a place where you will see it daily, serving as a gentle reminder of your healing journey and the support that surrounds you.

By embracing these healing practices, you not only mend the wounds of heartbreak but also reclaim your emotional space, ready to welcome new love and experiences with an open, healed heart. Remember, the magic you wield is born from your own resilience and capacity for renewal—tools that empower you to rise from the ashes of past pains, stronger and more whole than before. As you continue to explore these spells and rituals, let them be your companions on the path to healing, guiding you gently back to a place of peace and equilibrium.

4.4 COMMUNICATION ENHANCEMENT SPELLS FOR RELATIONSHIPS

In the intricate dance of relationships, the steps of communication play a pivotal role. Whether it's a romantic partnership, family ties, or friendships, the ability to convey thoughts and emotions clearly and to listen with empathy can transform superficial interactions into profound connections. Enhancing communication through spellwork not only improves your ability to express yourself but also deepens your understanding of others, fostering stronger, more meaningful relationships.

Spells for Honest Communication

A spell designed to foster honest communication can help remove barriers that might prevent openness in conversations. One effective spell involves the use of blue candles, as blue is the color associated with the throat chakra, which governs communication. Begin by setting a serene space, perhaps at a small altar or a quiet corner of your home, where you feel at ease. Place two blue candles in the center to represent yourself and the person with whom you wish to improve communication. As you light these candles, visualize a clear, bright light emanating from them, enveloping both of you. This light symbolizes a channel of clear, transparent communication. Use a feather to waft the smoke from the candles towards you and the imagined person, signifying the free flow of words and feelings. While doing this, chant softly, "Let honesty flow, let our true words show." Let the candles burn down safely, releasing your intention into the universe. Practice this spell prior to important discussions or whenever you feel that communication barriers are affecting your relationships.

Throat Chakra Balancing Rituals

Balancing your throat chakra is crucial for enhancing your communication skills. This chakra is the center of verbal expression and governs how effectively we communicate our thoughts and feelings. A balancing ritual can help clear any blockages in this chakra, improving your ability to speak and listen with clarity. Start this ritual by finding a quiet space where you won't be disturbed. Sit comfortably and hold a piece of aquamarine or turquoise, both of which are stones known to aid throat chakra healing. Close your eyes and take deep, slow breaths to center yourself. Visualize a bright blue light at your throat, spinning gently and growing brighter with each breath. As you focus on this light, imagine it expanding slowly, clearing out any fears or hesitations you have about speaking your truth. You might choose to use a mantra like, "I speak my truth clearly and listen with intent." Repeat this mantra softly, letting the words and the energy of the stone infuse your throat chakra with healing light. This ritual can be done regularly to maintain an open and balanced throat chakra, ensuring that your communication remains clear and effective.

Rituals for Listening and Understanding

Listening is just as important as speaking in any communication process. Enhancing your ability to listen deeply can greatly improve your relationships. A simple ritual to improve listening involves the use of a small, quiet water fountain or a bowl of water if a fountain is not available. Water is a symbol of fluidity and reflection, mirroring the flow of communication and the need for deep listening. Place the water element in front of you and sit quietly, allowing the sound of the water to fill your space. As you listen to the water, let it draw away the noise of your own thoughts, clearing a space for you to receive words and feelings from others. Hold a stone like blue lace agate, which promotes calm and understanding, and focus on your intention to listen not just with your ears, but with your heart. This practice can be particularly helpful before engaging in conversations where active listening is essential.

Herbs and Crystals for Communication

Incorporating specific herbs and crystals into your communication spells can enhance their effectiveness by aligning your energetic field with the energies of clear expression and understanding. Herbs like lavender and chamomile can be used to calm nervous energy, making it easier to express yourself clearly. You might create a small sachet of these herbs to carry with you or place them around your communication spaces. Crystals such as sodalite and blue topaz are excellent for enhancing communication. Sodalite strengthens self-expression and confidence, while blue topaz is known to sharpen intelligence and reduce misunderstandings. Carry these crystals with you, wear them as jewelry, or place them near your communication spaces to help facilitate clearer and more effective exchanges.

By engaging in these spells and rituals, you actively enhance your ability to communicate openly and honestly, listen deeply, and understand others more completely. This not only enriches your personal relationships but also contributes to a more empathetic and connected world. As you continue to use these magical tools, observe the subtle yet profound shifts in your interactions and revel in the clarity and depth that enhanced communication brings to your relationships.

4.5 PROTECTING YOUR EMOTIONAL SPACE: SPELLS FOR BOUNDARIES

In the dance of daily interactions, maintaining one's personal emotional space is not just a luxury but a necessity for well-being. This is particularly true in relationships where the exchange of energy is constant and sometimes overwhelming. Crafting spells for setting and maintaining healthy emotional boundaries helps you navigate this space safely, ensuring that while you connect with others, you do not lose yourself in the process. A foundational spell for establishing boundaries involves the use of candles and visualization, elements common in many magical practices for their simplicity and effectiveness. Choose a black candle for protection and a white candle for purity and spiritual strength. Place these candles on your altar or in a safe space where you can focus without interruption. As you light each candle, visualize a circle of light forming around you, signifying the boundary that protects your emotional space. With each breath, see this circle become brighter and more solid, allowing only those energies that are for your highest good to enter. Speak aloud your intention to maintain this boundary consistently, using words that affirm your right to emotional safety, such as, "I surround myself with safe and nurturing interactions, and my emotional space is protected." This ritual not only sets a clear boundary energetically but also reinforces your mental commitment to safeguarding your emotional well-being.

For those who identify as empaths or those particularly

sensitive to the emotions of others, protection spells specifically designed to shield against emotional overwhelm can be invaluable. Empaths often absorb feelings from those around them, which can lead to emotional overload if not managed carefully. A protective spell for empaths might involve creating a protective amulet using crystals known for their shielding properties, such as black tourmaline or hematite. Begin by cleansing your chosen crystal with salt water or sage smoke to clear any preexisting energies. Hold the crystal in your hand and charge it with your intention to block unwanted energies. You might say, "I am protected from emotional overwhelm, and I retain my own energy." Carry this crystal with you, especially in situations where you know you will be in crowded or emotionally charged environments. This small talisman acts as a shield, absorbing and repelling energies that might otherwise overwhelm you.

Self-preservation is crucial in relationships, especially in those dynamics where giving and receiving are not balanced. Rituals focused on self-preservation help maintain a healthy self-regard and emotional resilience, enabling you to engage with others from a position of strength and equilibrium. One such ritual involves the use of sea salt, a natural purifier, and water, an element associated with emotion. Fill a bowl with water and add three tablespoons of sea salt, stirring until dissolved. Dip your fingers into the bowl and sprinkle the salt water at the entrance to your home, your bedroom, and any other space where you spend a significant amount of time. As you do this, visualize a barrier that prevents negative energies from passing through. Chant a simple affirmation like, "My spaces are sanctuaries, I am restored here." This ritual not only cleanses your physical spaces but also sets a clear intention that your personal areas are places of renewal and emotional safety.

Creating and charging amulets and talismans to maintain personal boundaries is another effective way to ensure your emotional space is respected. These personal power objects serve as constant reminders of your boundaries and are imbued with your protective energy. To create a boundary amulet, choose items that symbolize protection and personal strength for you, such as a piece of obsidian for grounding and protection, a feather to symbolize freedom, or a piece of rosewood for protection against negative energies. Assemble these items in a small pouch, consecrate each by passing them through incense smoke, and speak your intention over them, such as, "I am strong, my boundaries are impenetrable." Carry this amulet with you, or place it under your pillow at night. Whenever you feel your boundaries being challenged, hold the amulet to remind yourself of your strength and the protective barriers you have set.

By incorporating these practices into your magical repertoire, you affirm your right to a healthy emotional life free from unwanted intrusions. Whether through spells, rituals, or the creation of charged objects, you take active steps to protect and preserve your emotional space, ensuring that your interactions are healthy, balanced, and nurturing. This proactive approach not only enhances your personal well-being but also empowers you to engage more fully and authentically in all your relationships.

4.6 CELEBRATING LOVE: SPELLS FOR PARTNERSHIP AND COMMITMENT

Amidst the ever-turning wheel of life, celebrating the love and commitment within our partnerships can be a profound source of joy and strength. Whether marking years of togetherness or nurturing the fresh blooms of a new relationship, the magic we weave to honor and strengthen these bonds holds a special place in the craft of witchcraft. Delving into spells that celebrate partnership, you'll find enchanting ways to not only mark these occasions but to deepen the connection and commitment that form the bedrock of your relationship.

Spells for Celebrating Partnership

Celebrating the journey you share with your partner can be both magical and meaningful. A beautiful spell to honor this partnership involves creating a love and commitment jar. Begin by finding a small, attractive jar and fill it with symbols of your relationship: photographs, love letters, or small mementos that hold special meaning. Intersperse these with lavender for calm, rose petals for passion, and basil for harmony. Seal the jar with red wax to symbolize your enduring love and speak your intentions of love and commitment into the jar as you seal it. Place this jar in the heart of your home, perhaps by the bed or on a shared altar, as a physical representation of your commitment to nurture and cherish the bond you share. This spell acts as a daily reminder of your journey together, reinforcing the love that grows and evolves each day.

Anniversary Rituals

Anniversaries and significant milestones offer a special opportunity to reinforce the magic of your partnership. A ritual to celebrate these moments might involve crafting a circle of love and gratitude. On the eve of your anniversary, create a circle with candles around the space where you and your partner will celebrate. Choose colors that resonate with love and commitment, such as pink for affection or green for growth. As you light each candle, share a memory or a reason for your gratitude towards your partner, allowing the warmth of your words to fill the space. This circle becomes a sacred space of shared memories and mutual appreciation, enhancing the bond and deepening the love between you both. This ritual not only marks the anniversary in a deeply personal way but also weaves a renewed commitment into the fabric of your relationship.

Commitment Rituals for New Relationships

In the tender beginnings of a new relationship, setting intentions for commitment and growth can lay a strong foundation for the future. A simple yet powerful ritual for this is the planting of a love tree. Together with your partner, choose a sapling that represents the qualities you wish to grow in your relationship—perhaps an oak for strength or an apple tree for sweetness. As you plant the sapling, each of you should place a stone at its base, inscribed with your intentions for the relationship. Water the tree with water mixed with honey, symbolizing the sweetness you hope to cultivate. As the tree grows, so too will your relationship, rooted in the intentions you've set and nurtured by the love and care you both invest. This ritual not only symbolizes the growing commitment between you and your partner but also serves as a living reminder of your shared intentions and dreams.

Harmony and Unity Spells

Creating harmony and unity within a relationship ensures that both partners feel valued and understood. A spell to promote this harmony involves the crafting of a harmony sachet, which both partners keep. Fill two small bags with herbs that foster understanding and peace, such as chamomile for tranquility and sage for wisdom. Add a small piece of amethyst to each, known for its ability to promote balance and peace. As you each carry your sachet, it serves as a gentle reminder of your mutual respect and the importance of maintaining harmony within your relationship. This simple spell helps smooth over rough edges and ensures that both partners remain attuned to the needs and feelings of the other, promoting a lasting and loving partnership.

~

As this chapter closes, reflect on the spells and rituals shared here, each a strand in the greater weave of your magical practice. Celebrating love, whether marking anniversaries, fostering new commitments, or enhancing harmony, enriches not only our personal lives but also strengthens the bonds that tether us to one another. As we transition from the magic of relationships to exploring the broader spiritual connections that shape our practice, remember that each spell cast and ritual performed is a testament to the transformative power of love and commitment in our lives.

CHAPTER 5

MASTERING ELEMENTAL MAGIC FOR PERSONAL USE

A s you deepen your journey into the realm of witchcraft, mastering the elements becomes a pivotal chapter in your magical education. Each element brings its own unique energy and properties, offering a diverse toolkit for personal transformation and empowerment. Among these, fire stands out for its dynamic and transformative power. Often associated with passion, purification, and renewal, fire magic is a potent ally in your quest for personal change and the manifestation of your deepest desires.

5.1 FIRE MAGIC: SPELLS FOR PASSION AND TRANSFORMATION

Harnessing Fire for Inner Change

Imagine standing before a crackling fire, feeling the

heat on your face and watching the flames dance with wild abandon. In this ancient and mesmerizing sight lies the key to personal transformation. Fire, with its raw energy and undeniable presence, is a powerful symbol of change. It consumes the old, making way for new growth and possibilities. To harness this transformative power, consider performing a simple fire meditation. Light a red candle, the color of passion and vitality, and sit comfortably in front of it. As you gaze into the flame, visualize the fire burning away any negative habits or burdensome past experiences, clearing the path for new opportunities and personal growth. This meditation not only aligns you with the element of fire but also ignites your inner passion, fueling your drive toward personal transformation.

Candle Magic for Beginners

Candle magic is one of the most accessible forms of spellwork, harnessing the elemental power of fire to manifest intentions. If you are new to this practice, start with understanding the basics, such as color correspondences and flame reading. Each color candle represents different energies and intentions: red for passion, blue for healing, green for prosperity, and so on. Begin your practice by choosing a candle color that aligns with your current desire or goal. As you light the candle, focus your intention into the flame, imagining your desire being transformed into light and energy. Watching the flame's behavior can also provide insights; a steady flame signifies strong and focused energy, while a flickering or dancing flame might suggest playful or scattered energies at work. This practice not only introduces you to the basics of elemental magic but also helps you connect more deeply with the energetic flow of your spells.

Spells for Career Advancement

Fire magic can be particularly effective in spells related to career advancement, where qualities such as ambition, determination, and action are crucial. A simple spell to boost your career involves writing your professional goals on a bay leaf, a herb associated with success and achievement. Light a yellow candle for intellect and clarity, and burn the bay leaf in its flame. As it burns, visualize your career path unfolding with the smoke, rising and expanding into the universe. This spell not only sets a clear intention for your career growth but also utilizes the motivating energy of fire to propel your professional life forward.

Rituals for Letting Go

Just as fire transforms wood into ash, it can symbolically burn away unwanted past experiences and negative habits. If you're holding onto something that no longer serves you, a fire ritual can be a powerful way to release it. Write down what you wish to release on a piece of paper—be it a bad habit, a painful memory, or an old grievance. In a fire-safe container, light the paper on fire, carefully watching as it turns to ash. As it burns, imagine letting go of these burdens, feeling lighter and freer with each flicker of the flame. This act of release not only clears your emotional landscape but also makes space for new, positive experiences to enter your life.

By engaging with fire magic, you tap into a primal force that has been revered and utilized in spiritual practices throughout history. Whether you are seeking inner transformation, career advancement, or the release of past burdens, fire provides the necessary energy to turn intention into reality. As you continue to explore and integrate this powerful element into your magical practice, remember that like the flame, your inner power is bright, dynamic, and capable of transforming anything it touches.

5.2 WATER MAGIC: SPELLS FOR EMOTIONAL HEALING AND INTUITION

Water, with its serene and flowing nature, naturally lends itself to spells and rituals designed to soothe emotions and enhance intuition. Embracing water magic allows you to tap into the deep currents of your psyche, uncovering insights and achieving emotional equilibrium. The fluidity of water is much like the fluidity of our emotions, capable of moving from calm to stormy with little warning. By learning to work with water, you gain the ability to balance these shifts and harness the profound reflective properties of this element.

Utilizing Water for Emotional Balance

Consider water's inherent qualities: it is adaptive, ever-changing, and reflective. These characteristics make it an ideal medium for spells focused on emotional healing. To create a spell that leverages water for emotional balance, begin by drawing a bath as a form of ritual cleansing. The bath serves as your sacred space, a container for your emotions and intentions. As you fill the tub, add sea salt to purify and protect your energy, and consider adding drops of calming essential oils like lavender or chamomile to enhance the soothing properties of the water. As you immerse yourself, close your eyes and visualize the water drawing out the negative emotions and stress, washing them away and leaving you centered and at peace. Use this time to meditate on the fluidity of water, reminding yourself that just as water flows around obstacles, you, too, can adapt and move past life's challenges.

Bath Spells for Self-Care

Bath spells are a cornerstone of water magic, providing a powerful way to combine hydrotherapy with spellwork. For stress relief, prepare a bath with Epsom salts to relax your muscles and clear your aura. Add a few drops of rose oil to elevate your mood and a handful of chamomile flowers to soothe your spirit. As you soak, focus on releasing any tensions or worries into the water, trusting in its capacity to absorb and transform your stress into tranquility. To enhance psychic intuition, incorporate botanicals like mugwort or jasmine into your bath. These herbs are associated with psychic powers and can help open your third eye, deepening your intuitive abilities. Light a purple candle nearby to symbolize spiritual insight, and as you relax in the bath, allow your mind to open to the subtle energies around you, receiving any messages or visions that might surface.

Moon Water for Enhancing Intuition

Moon water is a magical tool charged with the energy of the moon, particularly potent for spells involving intuition and psychic abilities. To create moon water, fill a clear glass container with natural spring water and set it outside under the light of a full moon. As the moonlight infuses the water, it charges it with lunar energy, known for its connection to intuition and the subconscious. After the water has charged overnight, use it to cleanse your magical tools, anoint your forehead before divination practices, or simply drink it to internalize the moon's qualities of insight and clarity. This practice not only strengthens your intuitive abilities but also connects you deeply with the lunar cycle, reminding you of the natural rhythms that influence our spiritual practices.

Water Scrying for Insight

Scrying is an ancient divinatory practice that involves gazing into a reflective surface to receive psychic visions or insights. Water scrying utilizes a bowl of water as this reflective surface, providing a medium through which you can tap into your subconscious mind. To practice water scrying, fill a dark bowl with water and add a few drops of ink to create a more reflective surface. In a dimly lit room, sit before the bowl and allow your gaze to soften, looking into the water but focusing on your inner intuitive voice. As images or symbols appear in your mind's eye, take note of them without judgment, allowing the water to guide your vision. This practice can be particularly revealing, offering insights into your emotional landscape or glimpses of future possibilities guided by the fluid and transformative nature of water.

Through these practices, water magic serves as a gentle yet powerful tool in your magical repertoire, ideal for nurturing your emotional health and enhancing your psychic senses. As you continue to explore and integrate water into your rituals, remember its lessons of adaptability and reflection, qualities that enhance not only your magical practices but also your everyday life.

5.3 AIR MAGIC: SPELLS FOR MENTAL CLARITY AND COMMUNICATION

In the realm of elemental magic, air is synonymous with the breath of life; it is the unseen force that pervades our existence, whispering ancient secrets and wisdom. The element of air is intrinsically linked to the mind, communication, and mental clarity. By learning to work with air, you engage with the flow of information and the movement of thoughts, clearing mental fog and enhancing your communicative abilities in profound ways. One effective method to harness the power of air is through focused breathwork combined with visualization. This practice can significantly clear mental blocks—an essential first step before any important communication or decision-making process. Begin by finding a quiet space where you can sit comfortably without disturbances. Close your eyes and take deep, measured breaths, drawing in the air slowly and exhaling any tension or clutter in your mind. Visualize this air as a bright, cleansing wind sweeping through your mind's corridors, clearing out cobwebs and dust that have settled over your thoughts. As your mind clears, imagine it as a vast, open sky, expansive and free of limits. This visualization not only calibrates your mental state but also aligns you with the element of air, enhancing your capacity to think and communicate clearly.

Feather Magic for Messages

Feathers, often considered gifts from the sky, carry with them the essence of air and its associated attributes of swiftness and elevation. In the practice of air magic, feathers can be used as potent tools for sending messages and receiving guidance from the spiritual realm. To utilize feather magic, select a feather that resonates with you—perhaps one that you've found on a walk or one gifted to you by a bird. Hold the feather in your hands and whisper to it your message or question for the spirits. When you feel ready, release the feather into the air from a high place, allowing it to carry your messages to the spiritual realms. As the feather dances with the wind, visualize your words traveling with it, reaching the ears of spirit guides or deities. This practice not only sends out your intentions but also opens a channel for receiving divine wisdom, which might come to you in the form of intuition, dreams, or signs.

Wind Spells for Change

Just as a strong gust can rearrange the landscape,

spells that call upon the wind can bring about significant change and help remove obstacles in your path. To perform a wind spell, choose a breezy day and find a spot where you can feel the wind's presence. Write down the changes you wish to manifest or the obstacles you need to remove on pieces of paper. One by one, hold these papers up to the wind, allowing the force of the air to snatch them from your fingers. As each paper flies away, visualize the wind carrying away the obstacles or swiftly bringing the desired changes into your life. This act of releasing your intentions to the power of the wind not only delegates the heavy lifting to the element of air but also symbolizes your trust in the natural forces to aid in your magical workings.

Smoke Cleansing for Purification

Utilizing the air element in purification rituals, particularly through smoke cleansing, is a practice steeped in tradition across various cultures. This technique involves burning sacred herbs or incense and using the smoke to cleanse a space, object, or person of negative energies. To perform a smoke cleansing ritual, light a bundle of dried sage, cedar, or sweetgrass, allowing it to smolder and produce smoke. Gently wave the smoke around the area or object you wish to cleanse, using a feather to help disperse the smoke more evenly. As you do this, visualize the smoke absorbing negativity and chaos, leaving behind only peace and purity. This practice not only clears the physical and energetic space but also invites freshness and clarity into the environment, making it an ideal preparation for any magical work or as a routine cleansing method to maintain a sacred space.

By weaving these practices into your daily life and magical routines, you deepen your connection with the element of air, enhancing your abilities in communication, mental clarity, and change. Embrace the lightness and agility of air, and let it lift you to new heights in your spiritual and magical explorations.

5.4 EARTH MAGIC: SPELLS FOR GROUNDING AND PROSPERITY

Earth, often regarded as the ultimate symbol of stability and nurturing, provides grounding and enriching energies that are essential for anyone seeking balance and abundance in their life. By connecting with the earth, you can harness its profound grounding properties, which help stabilize your energy and prepare you for prosperity and protection rituals. A deeply nurturing grounding ritual involves directly engaging with the soil, a practice known as earthing. Start by finding a quiet spot outdoors where you can safely and comfortably sit or stand barefoot on the ground. As you make contact with the earth, close your eyes and visualize roots extending from the soles of your feet deep into the soil. Imagine these roots drawing up the earth's energy, feeling it rise through your body, stabilizing and strengthening your core. Breathe deeply, inhaling the rich scents of the soil and the surrounding vegetation, each breath deepening your connection to the earth. This practice not only grounds your energy but also aligns you with the rhythm of the natural world, enhancing your overall well-being and spiritual balance.

Expanding your practice to include plant and tree magic can significantly enhance your ability to attract prosperity. Trees and plants are not merely passive elements of the landscape; they are active energy conduits that can amplify your magical workings. To attract abundance, consider working with a money tree plant, which as per folklore, can draw wealth into a home. Place the plant in the southeast corner of your home or office, an area often associated with prosperity. Water the plant regularly while visualizing your financial goals manifesting with each drop. Speak affirmations of abundance to the plant, such as "I am open and ready to receive all the wealth life offers." By nurturing the plant, you're symbolically nurturing your financial ambitions, allowing them to take root and grow.

Creating crystal grids is another powerful method for manifesting desires through the stabilizing energy of the earth. A crystal grid is an arrangement of crystals, often in geometric patterns, that combines their energies to support a specific intention. To create a grid for manifestation, select crystals like citrine for abundance, green aventurine for luck, and pyrite for prosperity. Arrange these crystals in a grid on a wooden or earthy base, such as a slice of a tree trunk or a ceramic plate. Place a clear quartz crystal at the center to amplify the energies of the surrounding stones. As you set up your grid, focus intensely on your intention, perhaps visualizing your desires coming to fruition. Activate the grid by tracing an imaginary line between the crystals with a wand or your finger, essentially connecting the dots to unleash the combined energy of the crystals toward your goal. This grid serves as a focal point for your intentions, continuously radiating energy into your space and drawing your desires into reality.

Lastly, the creation of earthen shields for protection incorporates the element of earth to safeguard both your physical and energetic space. One effective method is to create a barrier of salt, a mineral of the earth, around your home. Salt is known for its purifying and protective properties. To do this, sprinkle a line of sea salt across your doorways and windowsills, envisioning a barrier that blocks negative energies from entering. For added strength, you can also bury four quartz crystals at the corners of your property, setting an intention for each to protect your home. Another approach involves planting protective herbs like rosemary and thyme in your garden or near your entryways, as these plants are not only physically grounding but are also believed to offer spiritual protection. By integrating these practices into your routine, you create a robust shield that grounds and protects your personal space, harnessing the nurturing qualities of the earth to maintain a safe and harmonious environment.

5.5 SPIRIT AND THE FIFTH ELEMENT IN MODERN WITCHCRAFT

When we speak of the elements in witchcraft, often we recount the physical—earth, air, fire, water. Yet, there is a fifth, less tangible but equally powerful, known as Spirit or Aether. This element isn't just an absence of the physical; it represents the unseen forces, the energy that infuses all things, the breath of the universe that connects all. Spirit in witchcraft is the quintessence, the vital force that animates and brings magic to life. Engaging with Spirit in your rituals isn't merely an addition to your practice—it's a profound deepening, a way to tap into the raw essence of magic itself.

Connecting with Spirit during rituals involves recognizing this force as a living, breathing presence that can be invited and honored within your sacred spaces. Start by setting a clear intention to open yourself to the energy of Spirit. This can be as simple as stating aloud your desire to connect or as elaborate as a chant or poem that expresses your openness to divine guidance. As you perform your ritual, visualize a luminous energy surrounding and infusing your magical workings, a light that connects you to the universe's vast web. This visualization not only enhances your ritual's power but also aligns your spirit with the greater forces at play, providing a gateway for the divine to enter your practice. Using tools like quartz crystals can amplify your connection to Spirit, as they are known conduits of energy and intention. Place these crystals around your ritual space or hold one as you meditate, focusing on the flow of energy through the crystal and into the cosmos.

The role of ancestors and spirit guides is indispensable when discussing the element of Spirit. These entities are thought to be our link to the spiritual realm, acting as guardians and advisors in our magical practice. Working with them can enhance your understanding of Spirit and provide direct guidance on how to incorporate this element into your rituals. To connect with your ancestors or spirit guides, create an altar dedicated to them. Include personal mementos, photographs, or items they cherished in life to attract their attention and energy. Light a candle and offer some incense as symbols of the element of Air, inviting clarity in communication. As you call upon your ancestors or guides, be clear in your requests for guidance, and listen with your inner senses—intuition, emotions, thoughts— for any messages they might impart. Keep a journal nearby to jot down any insights or feelings that arise during these communications, as these can often be subtle and easy to overlook.

Integrating Spirit into elemental magic involves recognizing and utilizing this element as the binding force among the other four. When casting a spell or performing a ritual that involves multiple elements, invoke the element of Spirit to unify and amplify the energies present. For example, if you are conducting a spell for protection that involves earth (salt or herbs), water (a chalice of consecrated water), air (incense), and fire (candles), add an invocation of the Spirit as a way to harmonize these energies. You might say something like, "Spirit, who binds and animates all, I call upon you to unify these elements for my protection." Visualize a radiant light emanating from the center of your ritual space, linking each element in a circle of divine energy, strengthening and elevating your magical work.

Lastly, creating a sacred space that honors the element of Spirit transforms your regular practice area into a nexus for powerful magical work. This space should be a place where the physical meets the divine, where the boundaries between worlds soften, allowing for a seamless flow of energy. Use items that represent the spiritual to you—perhaps symbols of your spiritual path, statues of deities, sacred texts, or even elements from nature that you feel connect you to the divine. Arrange these items in a way that feels harmonious and inviting. Regularly cleanse this space with smoke or sound, reaffirming its sacredness and your commitment to maintaining it as a bridge between the seen and unseen worlds. As you spend time in this space, whether for daily meditations, spellwork, or simply to find peace, you reinforce its power as a sanctuary not just in your home but in your spiritual practice as well, making it a true embodiment of the Spirit element in your life.

5.6 ELEMENTAL BALANCE: CREATING HARMONY IN YOUR PRACTICE

In the vibrant tapestry of elemental magic, achieving a harmonious balance among the elements—earth, air, fire, water, and spirit—is crucial for enhancing your personal well-being and amplifying the effectiveness of your magical practices. Just as nature thrives on a balance of these fundamental forces, so too does your personal energy field. When one element dominates or another dwindles, it can lead to a sense of imbalance that might manifest as emotional upheaval, mental fog, or a lack of energy. To maintain an equilibrium that resonates with your intrinsic nature, it's essential to regularly assess and adjust your elemental alignment.

Assessing Elemental Balance

To begin assessing your elemental balance, take a moment to reflect on your recent experiences and feelings. Consider keeping an elemental journal where you record daily observations related to each element's presence in your life. Ask yourself questions like: Have I felt overly emotional or unusually detached? Is my mind clear or cluttered with thoughts? Do I feel energized or lethargic? Responses to these questions can indicate which elements are currently in excess or lacking. Additionally, you can use divination tools such as tarot cards, assigning each suit to an element (Cups for water, Swords for air, Wands for fire, Pentacles for earth) to gain insights into your elemental state. A spread focused on your current elemental balance can reveal areas that may need attention and guide you in making adjustments to restore harmony.

Rituals for Elemental Equilibrium

Engaging in rituals that balance the elements within you can significantly enhance your sense of well-being and deepen your connection to your magical practice. A simple yet effective ritual involves using representative objects of each element—stones for earth, incense for air, candles for fire, and a bowl of water. Arrange these items on your altar or in a sacred space, forming a circle that represents the unity of the elements. As you sit at the center of this circle, meditate on drawing balanced energy from each element. Visualize earth's stability grounding you, air's clarity refreshing your mind, fire's vitality energizing your spirit, and water's fluidity healing your emotions. This practice not only helps in realigning your elemental energies but also serves as a powerful reminder of the interconnectedness of all aspects of your life and the natural world.

Incorporating Elemental Symbols

To maintain a constant state of elemental balance in your daily life, incorporate symbols of each element into your environment. These symbols act as reminders of the qualities each element represents, helping to align their energies within your space. For example, decorate your home or workspace with images or items linked to each element—seashells or a small fountain for water, crystals or potted plants for earth, wind chimes or feathers for air, and candles or lamps for fire. You might also wear jewelry that represents the elements, such as a ring engraved with elemental symbols or a bracelet made of mixed gemstones. These subtle yet powerful symbols serve as continual prompts to remain connected to the elemental energies, fostering a balanced environment conducive to both spiritual growth and personal well-being.

Elemental Magic and Seasonal Changes

Aligning your elemental practice with the changing seasons can profoundly enhance the relevance and power of your spells and rituals. Each season naturally embodies different elemental qualities—spring resonates with the earth's fertility, summer with fire's brightness, autumn with air's changeability, and winter with water's introspection. By tuning into these seasonal energies, you can tailor your magical work to align with the natural flow, enhancing both its effectiveness and your connection to the cycle of the year. For instance, focus on growth and grounding spells in the spring, passion and protection spells in the summer, communication and letting go in the autumn, and emotional healing and reflection in the winter. This practice not only enriches your magical repertoire but also embeds a deeper sense of rhythm and timing into your work, mirroring the ebb and flow of nature itself.

As you continue to weave the balance of the elements into the fabric of your daily life and magical practices, remember that this balance is not a fixed state but a dynamic equilibrium that shifts and evolves with you. Regularly engaging in assessment, ritual, and mindful incorporation of elemental energies helps ensure that your practice remains vibrant and attuned to both your needs and the rhythms of the natural world. This harmonious integration not only enhances your personal well-being but also deepens your connection to the universe, enriching your magical journey with every step.

~

As this chapter on elemental balance concludes, we turn our attention to the next phase of our exploration, where we will delve into the protective and defensive aspects of witchcraft. In this upcoming chapter, we will explore the tools and techniques for safeguarding ourselves and our spaces, ensuring that our journey in witchcraft is not only empowering but also secure.

CHAPTER 6

PROTECTIVE AND DEFENSIVE WITCHCRAFT

I n the realm of witchcraft, as in life, protection forms the bedrock of our sense of security and well-being. Imagine a shield, not of steel, but of energy, meticulously woven from your own intent and the natural forces at your disposal. In this chapter, we explore how you, as a modern witch, can craft this shield using amulets, talismans, and herbal charms—tools as ancient as they are effective. These practices are not just about safeguarding yourself from external energies; they're about affirming your space in the universe, declaring it sacred and worth protecting.

6.1 CRAFTING PROTECTIVE AMULETS AND TALISMANS

Designing Personal Amulets

Amulets are personal talismans that serve as protectors

and guardians in your daily life. To craft an amulet, begin by selecting materials that resonate with protective energy. Common choices include iron for strength, black tourmaline for grounding negative energy, and amber for its cleansing properties. The shape of the amulet also holds significance; circular amulets represent eternal protection, while pointed ones can symbolize the deflection of harm.

Next, incorporate symbols that hold personal or universal protective power. The pentagram, a symbol of the five elements—earth, air, fire, water, and spirit—encapsulated in an unbroken line, is widely regarded for its protective qualities. Engrave or paint these symbols on your chosen material, infusing each stroke with your specific intent for protection.

The consecration of your amulet is crucial. This ritual, ideally performed during a waning moon to banish negativity, involves passing the amulet through the smoke of sage or palo santo, elements known for their purifying properties. As you do this, vocalize your intentions, affirming the amulet's role as your guardian. This not only charges the amulet with energy but also aligns it closely with your personal aura, enhancing its effectiveness.

Empowering Talismans with Intention

Talismans, unlike amulets, are not just protective but are imbued with the power to change things. To empower a talisman, you must first charge it with your intention. This process begins with a clear definition of what you seek protection from—be it negative energies, harmful influences, or emotional disturbances.

Visualization is a powerful tool in this step. Hold the talisman in your hand, close your eyes, and picture a bright, protective light emanating from within it, growing stronger with each breath. As you focus, visualize the talisman creating a barrier around you, shielding you from harm.

Incorporating elemental energies can also amplify your talisman's power. For instance, if using a stone like obsidian, consider burying it in the earth overnight to ground and stabilize the energy it holds. Alternatively, passing it through the flame of a candle can invoke the purifying properties of fire, cleansing it of any lingering negativity.

Herbal Charms for Protection

Herbal charms are a delightful and natural way to carry protection with you. These charms typically involve small bags filled with herbs chosen for their protective properties. Consider lavender for peace, black pepper for banishing evil, and hyssop for purification. Mixing these herbs allows you to tailor the charm's energies to your needs.

To enhance the charm's potency, add a few drops of essential oils or small crystals. For example, a drop of rosemary oil can boost mental clarity and ward off confusion, while a small amethyst crystal might be used to guard against psychic attacks.

Maintaining the Power of Amulets and Talismans

The potency of protective items can diminish over time, making regular cleansing and recharging essential. Each full moon, place your amulets and talismans on a windowsill to bathe in the moonlight, rejuvenating their energies. Alternatively, burying them in the earth overnight allows them to discharge any absorbed negativity and recharge with the stabilizing forces of the earth.

Regularly check in with your protective items through meditation. Hold them in your hands and attune to their energies. This not only strengthens your connection with them but also alerts you to any changes in their energy, signaling when they might need cleansing or recharging.

Interactive Element: Reflective Journaling Exercise

Take a moment to reflect on the protective practices you've established. In your journal, note any new techniques or rituals you've incorporated from this chapter. How have they changed your sense of security or your daily practices? Noting these observations can be enlightening, showing you the tangible benefits of your protective magic and encouraging its regular use.

As we weave through the fabric of our magical practices, the creation, maintenance, and empowerment of protective items stand as a testament to our commitment to safeguarding our spiritual journey. These ancient tools remind us that we hold the power to define the energies that we allow into our lives and that through focused intent and ritual, we can maintain not just safety but a sacred space for our magical practices to flourish.

6.2 HOME PROTECTION SPELLS: SAFEGUARDING YOUR SACRED SPACE

Creating a sanctuary for yourself extends beyond comfortable furnishings and decor; it involves securing your space against any form of negative energy or intrusion. This protection not only fosters a stable environment for personal growth but also ensures your home remains a true haven of peace. Let's explore various methods—from boundary spells to plant magic—each designed to fortify your home's energetic security.

Boundary Spells for the Home

Imagine enveloping your home in a protective shield, much like casting a spell of invisibility against negativity and harm. One effective way to achieve this is through the use of salt, water, and crystals, each element bringing its own strength to the boundary. Start by mixing sea salt and water, infusing it with protective intentions. As you blend these elements, visualize them creating a barrier that repels unwanted energies. Sprinkle this saltwater solution around the perimeter of your home, focusing on doorways, windows, and other entry points. For enhanced protection, place black tourmaline crystals at each corner of your house. Known for their strong protective properties and ability to absorb negative energy, these crystals act as guardians, standing watch over your space. As you set each crystal, affirm your intention for protection, perhaps saying, "This home is shielded from harm; only love and peace may enter." This ritual not only sets a physical boundary but also aligns your home's energy with safety and peace.

Warding Rituals for Entrances

Your home's entrances are both welcome points for guests and potential vulnerabilities for energy breaches. To fortify these portals, consider implementing warding rituals that specifically focus on doors and windows. Begin by creating a protective paste using herbs like rosemary for purification and black pepper for banishment. Mix these herbs with salt and a small amount of water to form a paste. Use this mixture to draw symbols of protection, such as pentacles or protective runes, on the thresholds of your doors and windows. Each mark serves as a seal, guarding against the entry of any negative forces. As you apply the paste, visualize a bright, protective light emanating from the symbols, creating an impassable barrier. This ritual not only strengthens the energetic warding of your home but also serves as a reminder of your commitment to safeguard your sacred space.

Protective Sigils for Household Security

Sigils are powerful symbols imbued with specific intentions, and when used for protection, they act as constant guardians over your home. Designing protective sigils can be a deeply personal and creative process, allowing you to tailor the symbols to the specific needs of your household. To create a sigil, start by writing out your intention for protection in a simple statement. Then, reduce this statement down to its essential letters and artistically rearrange them into a symbol that resonates with you. Once your sigil is designed, activate it by visualizing it glowing with protective energy. You can then draw these sigils above doorways, beneath mats, or anywhere you feel needs safeguarding. For those less inclined towards drawing, small prints of your sigil can be placed around the home. These sigils work quietly yet powerfully, providing a layer of security that moves with the rhythms of your daily life, adapting and strengthening as needed.

Plant Magic for Home Protection

The natural world offers its own powerful tools for protection, and incorporating plant magic into your home serves both practical and mystical purposes. Certain plants are known for their protective qualities and can be strategically placed around your home to enhance its security. For instance, thorny plants like roses or hawthorn are traditionally believed to ward off negative energy and intruders when planted near windows or along the perimeter of your property. Inside, herbs like basil and lavender can be kept in pots to purify the air and promote a peaceful atmosphere. Each plant not only contributes to the aesthetic and air quality of your home but also stands as a living guardian, its very life force dedicated to protecting your space. As you care for these plants, acknowledge their role in your home's protection, perhaps offering them water charged with protective intentions or placing small stones at their base to amplify their energy.

Incorporating these protective practices transforms your home into a fortress of peace and positivity, shielding you from external negativity and allowing you to thrive within its walls. As you continue to explore and apply these spells and rituals, remember that the strength of your protections is directly linked to the clarity of your intentions and the depth of your convictions. Keep nurturing these energetic defenses, and they will, in turn, nurture and protect you.

6.3 PSYCHIC SHIELDING TECHNIQUES FOR EVERYDAY LIFE

In the bustling flow of daily life, where energies swirl around as diversely as the people you encounter, establishing strong psychic shields forms an essential part of maintaining your emotional and spiritual well-being. These shields act like invisible bubbles, safeguarding you from the myriad of energies that can affect your mood, energy levels, and overall peace of mind. Building these shields isn't just about protection; it's about creating a stable personal space that allows you to interact with the world without being overwhelmed by it.

Building Psychic Shields

To start building effective psychic shields, you must first ground yourself, which stabilizes your energy to prevent any psychic turbulence. A simple grounding technique involves visualizing roots extending from your feet deep into the earth, anchoring you firmly to the ground. Once grounded, envision a bubble forming around you, starting from your heart and expanding outward. This bubble is your primary psychic shield. Intend for this shield to act as a barrier against any unwanted energies. It helps to visualize the shield's texture and color—perhaps a bright, translucent blue that is both calming and protective. Layering your shield with reflective properties, imagining it as a mirror that bounces back negativity, can further enhance its protective strength. Practice this visualization regularly, especially before stepping into situations where negative energies might be prevalent, such as crowded public spaces or stressful work environments.

Visualization for Shielding

Enhancing your psychic shields through visualization exercises not only strengthens them but also makes them more resilient to psychic disturbances. Start by visualizing your shield as detailed above. Then, in your mind's eye, strengthen the shield by thickening its walls with every inhale, drawing in positive energy, and with every exhale, reinforcing the shield's boundaries. Another powerful visualization involves imagining a bright light within you, growing in intensity and power. See this light expanding to fill your entire shield, solidifying it with the brilliance of your own energy. This light acts as a barrier that fine-tunes your shield, allowing only positive energies to penetrate while deflecting negativity. Regular practice of these visualizations can turn your psychic shields into a natural extension of your energy system, automatically activating when needed.

Empathic Protection Strategies

For those who identify as empaths, everyday interactions can sometimes feel like walking through an emotional minefield. The ability to absorb others' emotions, while a profound gift, can also lead to emotional overload if not managed properly. To protect your energy, it's crucial to have specific strategies in place.

One effective method is the 'zip up' technique, which involves visualizing a zipper running from the base of your spine to the top of your head. Imagine drawing this zipper up, sealing your energy field and protecting you from external emotions. Additionally, setting clear emotional boundaries is vital. Before entering potentially over-whelming situations, affirm to yourself what you are and are not willing to absorb. Mentally prepare yourself to encounter strong emotions and rehearse in your mind how you will protect your energy, perhaps by visualizing stepping back into your shield or mentally 'pushing' away negative energies.

Reinforcing Shields with Crystals

Crystals serve as powerful allies in reinforcing your psychic shields. Certain crystals, like black tourmaline and obsidian, are known for their protective properties, absorbing and neutralizing negative energies. Wearing these crystals as jewelry or carrying them in your pocket allows you to keep their protective energy close throughout the day. Placing these crystals at home or in your work-space can create a protective grid that shields you from psychic noise. For empaths, wearing a piece of labradorite can be particularly beneficial, as it not only protects but also strengthens the aura, preventing energy leaks. To maximize the effectiveness of these crystals, cleanse them regularly under running water or with sage smoke to ensure they remain energetically clear and potent. Make a habit of connecting with your protective crystals through meditation, holding them in your hands, and visualizing their energy merging with your psychic shields, enhancing your overall protection.

As you integrate these techniques into your daily practices, remember that psychic protection is not about building walls to keep the world out but about creating a filter that allows you to experience the world more fully, on your own terms. With these shields in place, you can navigate your day with confidence, secure in the knowledge that your energy is safeguarded, allowing your true self to shine through, uninhibited and strong.

6.4 SPELLCRAFT FOR NEUTRALIZING NEGATIVITY AND HEXES

In the intricate dance of energies that surround us, not all vibrations contribute positively to our spiritual ecosystem. Sometimes, despite our best efforts, we may encounter negativity or even targeted hexes. However, the power to cleanse these energies and reclaim our peace lies within our grasp through the practiced art of spellcraft. Let's explore some straightforward yet potent rituals aimed at neutralizing negativity, breaking hexes, and creating protective circles that guard our magical workings.

Neutralizing Negative Energy Spells

Imagine walking into a room and feeling an immediate heaviness, a leftover residue from a recent argument or negative encounter. To cleanse your space and self from such energies, a simple but effective spell involves the use of an elemental approach with water and salt, both known for their purifying properties. Begin by mixing sea salt into a bowl of water, imbuing it with your intent to cleanse and purify. As you stir the water, envision the salt absorbing the negative energies, just as it absorbs moisture. Sprinkle this holy water in corners of your room or wipe down surfaces where negative energy might linger. For personal cleansing, dip your fingers in the saltwater and lightly sprinkle some on your head, heart, and feet, visualizing the negativity washing away, leaving you refreshed and renewed. This ritual acts like a reset button, effectively dissolving the negative energies that cloud your environment and spirit.

Hex Breaking Rituals

Breaking a hex or curse demands not only power but wisdom and precaution, ensuring that you do not inadvertently harm yourself or others. If you suspect that a hex has been placed upon you, a ritual involving a reversal spell can be particularly effective. This involves creating a doll or effigy representing yourself made from natural materials like clay or cloth. As you construct the effigy, focus on it being a stand-in for you, absorbing the negative energies of the hex. Once completed, prepare a small fire in a cauldron or fire-safe container. Speak aloud your intention to reverse the hex, then carefully place the effigy into the flames, allowing it to be consumed by the fire. As it burns, envision the hex being neutralized, its power turning to ash. It is crucial during this process to maintain a clear focus on protection and purification, ensuring that the spell does not cross into the realms of harm or revenge.

Protection Circles for Spellcasting

When engaging in spellwork, especially of a protective or defensive nature, casting a protection circle provides a safe and sacred space for your magical endeavors. To cast this circle, gather four stones representing the cardinal elements—north (earth), east (air), south (fire), and west (water). Place these stones in their respective directions to anchor the circle. Stand at the center with a wand or simply use your finger to draw a visualized circle around you, connecting each stone with beams of protective light. As you draw, call upon the elements to guard and protect you, saying, "Elements of earth, air, fire, and water, form a shield around me, let no harm come within." With each invocation, imagine a wall of light being built around you, solidifying into an impenetrable barrier. This circle will protect you from external energies and interference, creating a pure and focused environment for your spellwork.

Creating Elixirs for Cleansing Negativity

Elixirs, infused with herbs and crystals, serve as potent tools for cleansing negativity from your aura or your home. To create a cleansing elixir, select herbs like sage for purification, rosemary for mental clarity, and lavender for peace. Place these herbs in a clear glass jar, and cover them with a carrier oil like almond or olive oil. Add a quartz crystal to amplify the mixture's cleansing properties. Seal the jar and allow it to sit in a sunny spot for a full day, letting the sunlight energize and infuse the elixir. Once ready, you can anoint doorways, windowsills, and other entry points in your home to cleanse incoming energies. For personal use, dab the elixir on your wrists, behind your ears, and over your heart, reinforcing your energetic cleanliness and protection. This elixir acts as a gentle yet powerful ally, keeping your spiritual pathways clear of lingering negativity.

6.5 CLEANSING RITUALS FOR PERSONAL AND SPACE PURIFICATION

Smudging and Smoke Cleansing

In the practice of witchcraft, the purity of your personal space and the energy around you is not just a preference; it's a necessity for maintaining balance and enhancing your magical workings. Smudging and smoke cleansing are age-old rituals that utilize the sacred smoke from burning herbs like sage, palo santo, or cedar to clear spaces of negative energies and create room for positive influences. To begin a smudging session, first open your windows and doors to allow an exit path for the unwanted energies. Light your chosen herb bundle or wood, and let it catch fire briefly before gently blowing out the flame to allow smoke to start billowing out. As the smoke rises, use your hand or a feather to guide the smoke into the corners of each room, under furniture, and around doorways, focusing on areas where the energy feels heavy or stagnant. As you do this, hold a clear intention in your mind to dispel negativity and purify the space. You might use a simple chant like, "Smoke of sage (or palo santo/cedar), cleanse this home of all impurity and negativity." Move methodically through your space, allowing the smoke to envelop each area thoroughly before concluding the ritual by expressing gratitude to the plant spirit for its protection and purification. This ritual not only refreshes your living space but also aligns it energetically with your spiritual goals.

Sound Cleansing with Bells and Chants

Sound is a powerful energy conductor, and in the realm of protective witchcraft, it can be a potent tool for cleansing and harmonizing spaces. The resonant tones produced by bells, singing bowls, or chants work by breaking up stagnant energy patterns, allowing fresh, vibrant energy to take their place. To cleanse a space with sound, begin by choosing a clear, resonant bell or a singing bowl. As you move through each room, ring the bell or play the bowl, focusing on areas that feel particularly dense or blocked. The sound waves create a vibration that penetrates these dense energies, breaking them apart and restoring flow. Chanting is another effective sound technique; you can use simple, repetitive phrases filled with your intention for peace and clarity, such as "Peace fills this room, all negativity is dispelled." The vibration of your voice not only helps to clear the space but also imbues it with your personal energy and intention, making it a deeply personalized ritual. Integrating sound into your cleansing rituals not only purifies the physical space but also elevates the spiritual atmosphere, making it conducive to healing and magical practices.

Water Cleansing Rituals

Water, with its intrinsic cleansing properties, is a natural choice for purification rituals. To harness these properties, create a cleansing solution by infusing water with salt—a powerful element known for its ability to absorb negative energies—and herbs like rosemary for protection and lavender for peace. Add a few drops of essential oils, such as eucalyptus or peppermint, to enhance the water's purifying effects. With your solution prepared, dip a clean cloth into the water and gently wipe down surfaces in your home, particularly those that see frequent contact such as door handles, countertops, and ritual tools. As you wipe, visualize the water absorbing all negativity, leaving behind a trail of sparkling, rejuvenated energy. For an added layer of spiritual cleansing, you can sprinkle this water around your home's perimeter or lightly spritz it in the air with a spray bottle, casting a fine mist of protective moisture. This method not only cleanses your physical space but also aligns it more closely with your spiritual vibrations, creating a sanctuary that supports your emotional and energetic health.

Light Cleansing Practices

The use of natural light, both sunlight and moonlight, for cleansing and recharging is a simple yet profoundly effective practice. To cleanse and energize your magical items, such as crystals, amulets, or ritual tools, place them outside under the direct light of the sun or the full moon for a few hours. The sun's powerful rays are particularly effective at purging accumulated energies, while the moon's gentle luminescence tends to recharge and enhance the mystical properties of your items. If placing items outside isn't feasible, positioning them on a windowsill where they can bask in the light also works well. As your items absorb the light, visualize them being infused with vitality and purity, ready to serve your magical needs with renewed strength. This practice not only ensures that your tools are energetically potent but also connects them more deeply with the natural cycles of the universe, enhancing their alignment with your spiritual path.

6.6 ETHICAL CONSIDERATIONS IN DEFENSIVE WITCHCRAFT

In the sphere of defensive witchcraft, where we weave spells and set boundaries to protect ourselves and our loved ones, ethical considerations form the bedrock of our practice. Adhering to the ethos of 'harm none' is paramount, not only to avoid unintended consequences but also to uphold the integrity of our magical path. This principle reminds us that the energy we send out into the universe has a way of returning to us, often magnified. Therefore, every protective spell or ritual we perform should be infused with the highest intentions, not only to safeguard ourselves but also to contribute positively to the cosmic balance.

Ethics of Protection and Defense

When considering the ethics involved in protective and defensive magic, it's crucial to reflect on the intent behind each spell or ritual. Protection doesn't mean harm to another—even if it's in response to a negative action. For instance, rather than crafting a spell that might bind someone else's will or direct misfortune their way, focus on strengthening your personal resilience and creating a shield that deflects negativity. This approach ensures that you're not contributing to a cycle of harm and retaliation but are instead fostering a cycle of strength and positivity. Visualization techniques can be particularly effective here; envision a shield of light surrounding you, repelling negativity without sending it back to its source.

Consent in Protective Spells

When performing spells intended to protect others, the importance of consent cannot be overstressed. Just as we respect physical boundaries, so too must we respect spiritual ones. Before you include someone else in your protective rituals, it's essential to obtain their explicit permission. This respects their free will and spiritual autonomy and ensures that your protective energies align with their personal energies, thereby enhancing the effectiveness of the spell. For example, if a friend is feeling vulnerable and requests a protection spell, discuss what they hope to achieve and any specific concerns they have, ensuring that the spell you craft aligns precisely with their needs and wishes.

Responsibility in Curse Breaking

Breaking curses or hexes is a serious undertaking that requires not only power but also wisdom and caution. It's vital to approach this with a clear and focused intention, fully aware of the responsibility that comes with such acts. Protecting yourself during this process is crucial; ensure you have strong protective measures in place, such as casting a circle of protection or carrying protective amulets.

When breaking a curse, focus your energies on dissolving the negative spell and healing its effects rather than retaliating against the one who cast it. This maintains the ethical stance of harm none and focuses on restoration and peace rather than continuing a cycle of negative energy.

Balancing Protection with Openness

Maintaining a balance between being protected and being open to positive experiences and energies is another nuanced aspect of defensive witchcraft. Over-guarding oneself can lead to isolation or a blockade against beneficial influences. It's important to fine-tune your protective practices so that they shield against negativity while still allowing positive interactions and energies to reach you. One way to achieve this balance is by regularly reassessing your protective shields and adjusting them based on current circumstances. If you find yourself feeling cut off from positive experiences, it might be time to soften your defenses slightly, visualizing them as selectively permeable rather than impenetrable.

Navigating the complexities of defensive witchcraft with ethical diligence ensures that your practices not only protect but also harmonize with the broader energies at play in the universe. By focusing on protection that harms none, obtaining consent where needed, handling significant spells like curse breaking with utmost responsibility, and maintaining a healthy balance between defense and openness, you embody the wise and ethical practitioner who uses their power for the greater good.

As we conclude this exploration of protective and

defensive witchcraft, remember that the strength of your magic lies not just in the spells you cast but in the ethical integrity with which you cast them. Each choice to protect, each decision to harm none, reinforces the positive impact of your magical practice, not just on yourself but on the wider world.

~

HAVING FORTIFIED our knowledge and practices around protection and defense, we now turn our attention to integrating magic more deeply into our everyday lives. In the upcoming chapter, we will explore practical ways to weave magic into daily routines, enhancing our living spaces and personal wellness through the subtle power of everyday magic. This natural progression from establishing strong defenses to creating a magically enriched daily life invites us to live fully in our power every single day.

CHAPTER 7
WITCHCRAFT IN DAILY ROUTINES AND SELF-CARE

Each day offers a fresh canvas, a new set of possibilities to infuse your life with magic and intention. Imagine waking up each morning not just to another day but to a magical opportunity, where every routine is a ritual and every chore a chance for enchantment. This chapter is dedicated to transforming your daily routines into moments of magical practice, enhancing your connection to your inner self and the universe through simple yet profound rituals.

7.1 MORNING RITUALS FOR A MAGICAL START TO THE DAY

Morning Affirmations and Intentions

The way we begin our mornings can set the tone for the entire day. Integrating morning affirmations and setting intentions are powerful practices that can transform ordinary mornings into extraordinary beginnings. Start by creating a set of affirmations that resonate deeply with your personal desires and aspirations. These might include statements like "I am aligned with the abundance of the universe" or "Today, I embrace my strength and wisdom." Speak these affirmations aloud as you stand in front of a mirror, making eye contact with yourself, reinforcing the connection between your spoken words and your internal belief system.

To enhance this ritual, incorporate a small candle-lighting ceremony where you light a candle as a symbolic gesture of bringing light—and insight—into your day. As the candle flickers, visualize your intentions spreading into the universe, mingling with the energies of all things and aligning external circumstances with your desires. This act not only sets a focused tone for the day ahead but also strengthens your manifestation skills, turning everyday morning routines into powerful spells for personal transformation.

Sunrise Rituals

Connecting with the sunrise offers a profound way to sync your personal rhythm with the natural world, celebrating the new day's potential. For a simple sunrise ritual, rise early and find a spot where you can clearly see the horizon. As the sun lifts above the horizon, stand with your feet firmly planted on the ground, your arms open wide, and breathe deeply. With each inhale, imagine golden sunlight filling your body, energizing and revitalizing every cell. With each exhale, release any remnants of yesterday, letting go of old energies and making space for new possibilities.

You can further enhance this ritual by holding a small crystal such as citrine or amber, which are associated with the sun's energy, to absorb and hold the light. Later, you can carry this crystal with you throughout the day as a reminder of the morning's intentions and energies, keeping you aligned and focused.

Cleansing Morning Showers

Transform your morning shower into a ritual of purification and protection. Begin by blessing your bathwater with intent, perhaps adding a pinch of sea salt for purification and a drop of essential oil like rosemary or lavender for clarity and calm. As you step into the water, envision it washing away any negative energies clinging to you, clearing your aura, and refreshing your spirit.

To deepen the ritual, you can chant or silently recite a mantra specific to your needs, such as, "Water flow, protect me from head to toe." Visualize a halo of protective light enveloping you as the water courses down, forming a shield that will guard you throughout the day. This practice not only cleanses your physical body but also fortifies your energetic field, preparing you for whatever the day may hold.

Breakfast Blessings

The first meal of the day is not just nourishment for the body but can also be an offering to your spirit. To bless your breakfast, begin by expressing gratitude for the abundance before you, acknowledging the earth, the growers, and the journey the food took to reach your table. As you prepare and plate your food, infuse it with intentions for the day— perhaps stirring your coffee clockwise to draw positive energy inward or arranging your fruit in a pattern that pleases your eye and spirit.

Before eating, pause for a moment to bless your meal. You might say, "May this food provide the strength, vitality, and joy I need for today." By imbuing your first meal with such intentions, you turn an ordinary activity into a sacred ritual, feeding not just your body but also your soul. This act of conscious eating sets a mindful tone for your day, reinforcing a state of awareness and gratitude that can lead to deeper spiritual connections and personal growth.

As we incorporate these morning rituals into our daily lives, each day becomes a new chapter in our journey of self-discovery and magical living. Each ritual, no matter how small, connects us more deeply to the magical potential within and all around us, empowering us to live more intentionally and joyously.

7.2 INCORPORATING MAGIC INTO DAILY SELF-CARE PRACTICES

Enchanted Skincare Routines

Transforming your daily skincare into a magical ritual not only enhances your natural beauty but also imbues your spirit with positive energies. Start by creating enchanted creams and homemade herbal infusions tailored to your specific skin needs and magical intentions. For instance, crafting a facial cream infused with rose petals can invoke love and self-acceptance, while chamomile might soothe both your skin and aura, promoting peace before you start your day.

To begin, select a base cream that suits your skin type—this could be a simple, unscented moisturizer from any health store. Next, choose herbs and flowers aligned with your intentions. For a calming night cream, lavender is perfect as it aids in relaxation and has beneficial properties for the skin. Steep the lavender in hot water to create a potent infusion, then mix this herbal water with your base cream. As you apply it, visualize the cream not only nourishing your skin but also forming a protective barrier that wards off negative energies.

Incorporate small rituals into your application process to deepen the magical experience. As you apply your enchanted cream, use gentle, upward strokes to lift your spirits and skin. Mirror work can be powerful here; look into your own eyes and affirm your worth and beauty. You might say, "With each touch, I am more radiant, inside and out." This practice turns a routine activity into a profound act of self-love and enchantment, setting a positive tone for your day or easing you into a peaceful night.

Magical Exercise Routines

Exercise is not just about maintaining physical fitness; it can also be a grounding and centering activity that aligns your body, mind, and spirit. To infuse your workout with intention and magic, start by setting a clear goal for each session. This might be something like cultivating strength, enhancing flexibility, or releasing stress. Whatever your focus, hold this intention clearly in your mind as you prepare.

Create a small ritual before you begin exercising. This could involve lighting a candle, laying out crystals associated with your intention, or even just taking a few deep, mindful breaths to center yourself. As you move through your exercise routine, visualize your intention with each movement. For instance, if your focus is on strength, imagine drawing the earth's energy up with each lift or push. Use affirmations to reinforce your intent, such as repeating, "I am strong, I am powerful," with each exertion.

Incorporating elements like music can also enhance your magical exercise routine. Choose songs that resonate with your intention, creating a playlist that motivates and uplifts you or calms and centers you, depending on your goals. The rhythm can help synchronize your movements and intentions, creating a flow that feels smooth and magical, transforming your exercise routine into a dance with the divine.

Mindfulness and Meditation

Integrating mindfulness and meditation into your daily life not only enhances your magical practices but also brings a deeper sense of peace and presence to your everyday activities. Start by choosing a regular time and place for your meditation—somewhere you can sit quietly without interruption. Morning might be ideal for setting a positive tone for the day or evening for unwinding and reflecting.

As you sit in meditation, focus on your breath to help anchor your mind. Breathe deeply and evenly, allowing your thoughts to flow without attachment. To enhance your practice, you might introduce a simple mantra or affirmation that aligns with your magical intentions, repeating it silently to help deepen your focus and manifest your desires.

Bringing mindfulness into your daily activities can transform tasks into magic. For example, as you cook, pay attention to the colors and textures of your food and the alchemy of the cooking process. Infuse your dishes with love and intention, turning each meal into a spell for nourishment and abundance. Or, while cleaning, visualize sweeping away not just physical dirt but also any negative energies, leaving your space bright and charged with positivity.

Journaling with Purpose

Magical journaling is a powerful tool for reflection, manifestation, and tracking your magical growth. To start, choose a journal that feels special—perhaps one with a beautiful cover or quality paper that inspires you to write. Dedicate a few minutes each day to this practice, choosing a quiet time where you can reflect without interruption.

In your journal, record your daily experiences, feelings, and insights related to your magical practice. Note any synchronicities or significant dreams, and reflect on the spells or rituals you perform. This not only helps you track your progress but also allows you to see the patterns and connections in your magical life, enhancing your under-standing and effectiveness.

To deepen the magical aspect of your journaling, you might incorporate sigils or symbols that represent your goals or achievements. You can also use colored pens to align with different intentions—green for growth, blue for healing, red for passion. Each entry then becomes a visual and energetic map of your journey, a living grimoire that not only documents your path but also actively contributes to your magical practice.

7.3 THE MAGIC OF MEAL PREPPING: KITCHEN WITCHERY FOR BEGINNERS

Imagine transforming your daily meal preparation into a practice of intention and energy, where every chop and stir infuses your food with more than just flavor, but with magic. In the heart of your home, the kitchen, you wield the power to turn everyday cooking into an act of spiritual nourishment. Infusing meals with specific intentions doesn't require grand gestures; rather, it's about the subtle incorporation of energy and focus into your culinary routines. Whether you're aiming to draw in love, usher in prosperity, or cultivate protection, the process begins the same: with the setting of a clear intention. Picture yourself preparing a meal for family or friends where the intention is to foster love and unity. Each ingredient, from the salt to the olive oil, is selected not only for its taste but for its ener-getic properties—salt for purification and grounding, olive oil for health and protection. As you mix these ingredients, visualize your love infusing the dish, imagine the laughter and warmth that will envelop the dining table, and hold onto these images as you cook, turning the act of meal preparation into a spell of affection and connection.

Herbal magic in cooking offers a delicious and easy way to incorporate the energies of the earth into your daily life. Herbs not only enhance the flavor of dishes but also carry their unique energies, which can be harnessed to align with your magical intentions. For instance, incorporating basil into a dish can attract luck and wealth, while adding rosemary can offer protection and mental clarity. To deepen your connection with these herbs, take a moment before adding them to your dish. Hold them in your hands, feeling their texture and inhaling their aroma. As you do this, communicate your intention to the herbs, whether it's a whisper or a focused thought, asking them to lend their strength to your purpose. Then, as you sprinkle the herbs into your cooking, visualize their energies combining with the food, transforming it into a vessel of your will. This practice not only imbues your meals with positive energy but also connects you more deeply with the natural world, enhancing your understanding and appreciation of the ingredients you work with.

Creating blessed beverages is another delightful way to weave magic into your daily life. Begin your day with a cup of tea or coffee that's not just a caffeine boost but a potion charged with your intention for the day. Let's say you need clarity and focus for a busy day ahead. Choose ingredients known for their mental-boosting properties, such as peppermint or green tea. As you boil the water, visualize it being charged with bright, sparkling energy. When you pour the water over your tea or coffee, see it as pouring clarity into your day. As you drink, imagine this clarity filling you, preparing you for the challenges ahead. This simple ritual turns your morning into a supportive magical practice, aligning your energy with your needs and intentions for the day.

The importance of creating a kitchen altar cannot be overstated in kitchen witchery. This sacred space serves as a focal point for your culinary magic, where you can store your magical tools—herbs, spices, and utensils—and where you can perform small rituals before beginning your cooking. Your altar might be a small shelf above your stove or a corner of your kitchen counter; what matters is that it is a place you regard with respect and significance. Decorate it with items that symbolize your magical practice: perhaps a statue of a deity associated with hearth and home or a candle to light when you begin cooking. This altar not only reinforces the sanctity of your kitchen as a magical workspace but also serves as a constant reminder of your connection to your craft. Each glance at your altar, each use of a tool stored there, reinforces your identity as a kitchen witch, weaving magic into every meal and stirring intention into every pot.

7.4 WITCHCRAFT ON THE GO: PORTABLE SPELLS AND PRACTICES

In the whirl of daily life, where routines can whisk you away from your sacred space, finding ways to maintain your magical practice on the go becomes essential. Whether you're commuting, traveling, or simply out and about, integrating portable spells and discreet magical objects ensures you stay connected to your witchcraft, no matter where your day takes you.

Travel Protection Spells

When setting out on a journey, whether for leisure or work, carrying a small, dedicated travel protection amulet can serve as a powerful safeguard. Crafting this amulet can be a simple yet profound ritual. Begin by selecting a small charm; a piece of turquoise is excellent for protection during travel and is known for its strength and healing properties. Infuse the stone with your intention through a small ritual. Hold the stone in your hand and visualize a shield of light enveloping you as you travel, protecting you from misfortunes and guiding you safely to your destination. You can enhance this spell by anointing the stone with a protective oil such as frankincense or myrrh, then carrying it in your pocket or as part of a piece of jewelry throughout your travels.

For verbal charms, consider crafting a short, memorable mantra that you can recite silently or aloud at the start of your journey. Something as straightforward as, "Guided and guarded, I travel safely" repeated three times can set a powerful protective spell in motion. This practice not only shields you physically but also aligns your energies with the flow of your travels, creating a smoother, more harmonious journey.

Discreet Spell Objects

Maintaining a magical connection discreetly throughout the day can be seamlessly achieved with small, inconspicuous objects imbued with your intent. A simple yet effective object could be a keychain adorned with symbols or stones significant to your practice. For example, a keychain featuring a small pentacle or a crystal like black tourmaline can serve as a discreet protective talisman. Another method involves carrying enchanted coins; these can be small, everyday coins that you have charged under the light of the full moon, carried in your wallet to attract abundance and prosperity.

Consider also the use of wearable magic in the form of jewelry. A bracelet strung with amethyst beads can be worn not only as an accessory but as a discreet way to enhance spiritual awareness and protection. Before wearing, hold the bracelet in your hands and charge it with a specific intention, perhaps using a simple affirmation like, "This amulet shields and supports me."

Quick Grounding Techniques

Staying grounded amidst the chaos of daily engagements is crucial for maintaining focus and balance. One quick and effective technique involves using your breath and visualization. No matter where you are, you can perform this technique by simply closing your eyes, taking a deep breath, and imagining roots growing from the soles of your feet deep into the earth. Visualize these roots drawing up stabilizing energy from the earth with each inhale, and with each exhale, release any stress or disarray you're experiencing. This can be done in just a minute or two, yet it profoundly re-centers your energy.

Another handy grounding method is to carry a small grounding stone, like hematite or smoky quartz, in your pocket. Whenever you feel unmoored, hold the stone and let its cool, steady texture remind you of the earth's enduring presence. Rubbing the stone between your fingers can help transfer the earth's stabilizing energies into your body, swiftly bringing you back to a state of balance.

Portable Altar Kits

For those who travel frequently or who enjoy performing rituals in various natural settings, a portable altar kit can be a sacred treasure. Start by selecting a small box or pouch that resonates with you. In it, place miniature versions of your typical altar items—a small candle, a tiny incense holder, a couple of small crystals, and miniature images or statues of deities or spirits you work with. You might also include a small cloth to lay out your items, transforming any space into a sacred one.

This kit allows you to set up a personal sacred space quickly, be it in a hotel room, a quiet corner of a park, or a temporary living space. It ensures that no matter where you are, you have the tools to engage with your practice, perform spells, or simply meditate and reflect. The act of unpacking and setting up your portable altar can itself be a ritual, affirming your commitment to your craft, regardless of your physical location.

By integrating these portable spells and practices into your life, you ensure that your connection to your magical practice remains constant and vibrant, no matter where life takes you. Each object, each charm, and each ritual becomes a thread in the woven tapestry of your daily magical practice, linking every moment of your day with intention, protection, and personal power.

7.5 CREATING A SACRED SPACE IN ANY ENVIRONMENT

Creating a sacred space isn't confined to vast, undisturbed corners of a home; it can flourish in the nooks of a bustling apartment or the corner of a shared room. The essence of a sacred space lies in its intention and the peace it brings to its creator. When working with small or shared environments, the key is adaptability and intention. Start by identifying a small area that you can dedicate to your practices — this could be a windowsill, a section of your desk, or a shelf. Focus on minimizing clutter in this area to maintain a clear, focused energy. Use small items that resonate deeply with you spiritually; a miniature statue, a small candle, or a few precious stones can effectively hold the energy of a larger altar. The placement of these items should be deliberate, each chosen and arranged according to what feels intuitively right for you, creating a focal point that draws you into a meditative, peaceful state whenever you gaze upon it.

Consider also the use of vertical space — hanging crystals in the window or wall-mounted shelves holding sacred objects can be especially beneficial in smaller settings. These elements not only save space but also elevate the energy literally and metaphorically. The light refracting through hanging crystals can cleanse the energy of the room each morning, filling your space with prismatic light that sets a serene tone for the day. This practice turns an ordinary part of your living area into a dynamic sacred space that interacts with the natural elements outside, bridging your inner sanctum with the outer world.

Mobile Sacred Spaces

For those who often find themselves on the move or those who cannot maintain a permanent altar, creating a mobile sacred space can be a game-changer. This can be as simple as a small box or pouch containing items that are spiritually significant to you — a piece of cloth to lay out as an impromptu altar cloth, a compact incense holder, a travel-sized candle, and perhaps a few small crystals or amulets. This portable kit allows you to establish a sacred space wherever you are, be it a hotel room, a garden, or during a quiet break at your workplace.

The act of setting up and taking down your portable altar can become a ritual in itself, marking the beginning and end of your sacred time. This ritual helps to mentally and energetically segregate your spiritual practices from your everyday routines, creating a temporary but powerful envelope of sacred space that travels with you. It serves as a physical reminder of your spiritual commitments and can be particularly comforting when you are away from home, providing a familiar anchor to your practice.

Incorporating Nature

In urban environments, maintaining a connection to nature, which is vital for many spiritual practices, can be challenging, but it is far from impossible. Integrating natural elements into your sacred space can help create a bridge to the natural world. Start with plants that resonate with your spiritual practice, herbs that you use in your magic, or plants that have particular significance in your spiritual path. Even in limited spaces, a small potted plant or a selection of herbs on a windowsill can serve as powerful symbols of life and growth.

Additionally, elements like small bowls of water, stones or shells collected from meaningful places, or even a jar of earth can be incorporated into your space. Each element brings the essence of nature into your sacred space, serving both aesthetic and energetic purposes. These elements act as touchstones to the natural world, grounding your practice in the energy of the earth and reminding you of the interconnectedness of all things.

Energetic Boundaries

Finally, ensuring that your sacred space remains energetically pure and protected is crucial, especially in shared or multifunctional areas. One effective way to create and maintain these boundaries is through the use of energy shields. Visualize a bubble or dome of light surrounding your sacred space, setting the intention that this barrier allows only positive, peaceful energy to enter. You can reinforce this barrier with physical representations, such as a ring of salt around your space or placing protective stones like black tourmaline at the corners of the area.

Regularly cleansing this space is also essential. This can be done by smudging with sage or palo santo, using sound from a bell or a singing bowl, or sprinkling moon water around the area. Each act of cleansing renews the energy and reaffirms the boundaries, ensuring that your sacred space remains a sanctuary for your spiritual practices. By engaging with your sacred space in these ways, you reinforce its significance and sanctity, making it a true source of strength and serenity in your daily life.

7.6 THE WITCH'S NIGHTLY RITUALS FOR REST AND REJUVENATION

Nighttime Protection Spells

As the sun sets and the world quiets, creating a protective ambiance in your home and around yourself ensures a night of peaceful and rejuvenating rest. Consider the night a time when you are most vulnerable, as your conscious guard is down during sleep. A simple yet effective spell involves the use of black tourmaline, a stone known for its protective and grounding properties. Place a piece of black tourmaline on each windowsill and by the main doorways of your bedroom or home. As you set these stones, visualize them forming a protective barrier that shields you from any unwanted energies or disturbances. Complement this with a nightly incantation, such as, "Shadows of the night, heed this call, around me now, protection wall." Recite this as you move through your space, reinforcing the boundary and settling your mind for sleep.

To enhance this protection, create a nightly ritual of lighting a specific candle—anointed with oils such as lavender and chamomile for relaxation and protection. As you light this candle, imagine it illuminating your space with a calming, protective glow. Let this candle burn safely in your room as you prepare for bed, filling the space with its gentle light and protective energy. This practice not only sets a tangible perimeter of safety but also fills your subconscious with reassurances of security, fostering a deeper, more restorative sleep.

Dreamwork Rituals

Dreams can be a powerful tool for self-discovery and spiritual communication. To harness the power of your dreams, incorporate dreamwork rituals into your nightly routine. Start by creating a dream sachet filled with herbs like mugwort and lavender, which are known to enhance psychic connection and promote relaxing sleep. Place this sachet under your pillow to stimulate insightful dreams and facilitate recall. Before sleeping, spend a few moments setting an intention for your dreams. You might focus on a question you need answers to or ask for guidance from your spirit guides or ancestors.

Upon waking, maintain a practice of jotting down your dreams in a dedicated dream journal. This not only helps in remembering your dreams but also in interpreting the symbols and messages they may contain. Over time, patterns may emerge that offer insights into your subconscious mind, aiding your spiritual growth and self-understanding. For those interested in lucid dreaming, where you become aware and can control your actions in the dream, begin practicing reality checks throughout the day—like reading digital numbers or looking at your reflection. These checks can carry over into your dreams, helping you gain lucidity.

Evening Reflection Rituals

Reflecting on the day's events is a crucial practice that allows you to process experiences and release any lingering negativity. Develop a ritual of sitting quietly each evening, perhaps with a cup of herbal tea, reflecting on the day's highs and lows. Use this time to acknowledge your feelings about various events, giving yourself space to feel and understand your emotions fully. This might involve writing in a journal or simply meditating on these thoughts.

A cleansing ritual can complement this reflection. Using a smudging stick, such as sage or palo santo, smudge around yourself and the space where you've spent your evening. As the smoke wafts around you, let it carry away any negative energy or stress, purifying your spirit. Conclude this reflection by setting an intention for the following day, focusing on positivity and growth. This not only clears your energy from the day's baggage but also aligns your spirit for the next day's challenges and opportunities.

Bedtime Blessings

Creating a restful sanctuary conducive to healing and deep sleep is essential. A bedtime blessing can be performed by anointing your bed with a few drops of a calming essential oil like lavender or chamomile mixed with moon water. As you sprinkle the water lightly over your bed, recite a blessing such as, "Bless this bed on which I lay, bring me peace till break of day." Feel the room fill with calming energies, preparing you for a night of healing sleep.

Consider the arrangement of your bedroom as well; ensure it feels open and restful. A clutter-free environment promotes a peaceful mind. You might add a small lavender plant or a calming piece of artwork that resonates with tranquility. These elements enhance the serene ambiance, making your bedroom a true haven for rejuvenation.

Incorporating these nightly rituals into your routine bridges the gap between day and night, ensuring that each transition is smooth and filled with intention. As you end each day with these practices, you not only protect your energy but also enhance your spiritual connection and personal growth, turning every night into an opportunity for deep spiritual nourishment and rest.

~

As we conclude this chapter on integrating witchcraft into daily routines and self-care, we recognize how each spell, ritual, and intentional act weaves deeper magic into the fabric of our everyday lives. From the moment we rise to the tranquility of night, our days are filled with opportunities for magical growth and personal empowerment. Moving forward, we'll explore the role of the witch in the modern world, expanding on how we can live out our truths in ever-expanding circles of light and community.

CHAPTER 8

THE FUTURE OF WITCHCRAFT: ETHICS, COMMUNITY, AND INNOVATION

I magine, if you will, a world where witchcraft continually evolves, seamlessly integrating the wisdom of the past with the innovations of the modern era. This chapter turns our focus toward the horizon of witchcraft, exploring how ethical practices, sustainability, and inclusivity are shaping the future of our craft. As we navigate these evolving landscapes, our commitment to ethical magic is more crucial than ever, ensuring that our practices not only honor the diverse tapestry of our global community but also contribute positively to the world around us.

8.1 THE ROLE OF ETHICS IN FUTURE WITCHCRAFT PRACTICES

Adapting Ethics for Modern Witchcraft

As witchcraft stretches its roots and branches across

diverse cultures and communities, the call for an evolved ethical framework becomes undeniable. Traditional principles like the Wiccan Rede, "An it harm none, do what ye will," have guided us well, but as our global footprint expands, so too must our ethical considerations. We find ourselves at a crossroads, seeking to balance age-old wisdom with contemporary concerns such as digital privacy, environmental impact, and cultural sensitivity.

In this modern context, ethics in witchcraft extend beyond spellcasting into the very materials and practices we employ. It demands of us a higher consciousness about the origins of our tools and ingredients, urging us to consider not just their magical properties but also the impact of their sourcing on communities and the environment. This heightened awareness leads us to favor ethically harvested herbs, sustainably mined crystals, and tools crafted from recycled or renewable resources, ensuring that our practices contribute to the healing, rather than the depletion, of the world.

Consent and Boundaries

The topic of consent in witchcraft, while always a cornerstone of ethical practice, has garnered a deeper dimension in today's interconnected world. It's about respecting personal boundaries and the autonomy of others in both physical and virtual spaces. Whether it's a healing spell for a friend or a protective charm for a loved one, the rule of thumb remains—consent is paramount. This respect for autonomy not only reinforces the integrity of our spells but also solidifies trust within the witchcraft community, fostering a safe and supportive environment for all practitioners.

Moreover, the concept of boundaries extends into the digital realm, where information is shared freely and often without thought to its implications. As practitioners, being mindful of what we share about our spells, rituals, and personal practices is crucial not only for our own privacy but also out of respect for the sacredness of our craft.

Sustainability in Spellcraft

Sustainability in witchcraft is not just a trend but a necessity, as the very essence of our practice is intertwined with the natural world. We draw our energies from the earth, air, fire, and water, and it is our duty to ensure that our practice does not harm these elements. Embracing eco-friendly practices—whether through using digital books of shadows to save paper, employing reusable spell components, or planting trees to offset the use of botanicals in our rituals—demonstrates our commitment to a harmonious relationship with the Earth.

This shift towards sustainable practices is not just about the physical aspects of witchcraft but also about fostering a sustainable mindset within our community. It involves educating new practitioners about the importance of ecological balance and encouraging seasoned witches to innovate and share their green practices, making sustainability a core principle of modern witchcraft.

Inclusivity and Diversity

Inclusivity and diversity are the cornerstones of the future of witchcraft. Our community is wonderfully diverse, encompassing practitioners from all walks of life, each bringing their unique perspectives, traditions, and energies. Embracing this diversity not only enriches our communal knowledge base but also deepens our collective magic, weaving a tapestry of practices that is as vibrant as it is powerful.

However, inclusivity goes beyond mere acceptance; it requires active engagement and willingness to learn from each other without appropriation. It involves creating spaces—both physical and digital—that are welcoming to all, regardless of background, identity, or tradition. It means crafting rituals that are adaptable to different needs and accessible to practitioners of all abilities, ensuring that everyone can participate in the magical community.

Interactive Element: Ethical Reflection Exercise

Consider the following questions to deepen your ethical understanding and application in your practice:

- How do I source my magical tools and ingredients, and what are their impacts on the environment and local communities?
- Do I seek consent and respect boundaries consistently in my magical and communal interactions?
- What steps am I taking to ensure my practice is sustainable and supports ecological balance?
- How do I promote inclusivity and diversity within my practice and the broader witchcraft community?

Reflecting on these questions not only helps you align your practice with modern ethical standards but also encourages a proactive approach to the evolving challenges and opportunities within witchcraft. As you ponder these questions, remember that ethics are not static; they require ongoing examination and adaptation as we continue to grow and learn within our magical practices and community interactions.

8.2 BUILDING COMMUNITY IN MODERN WITCHCRAFT

The fabric of modern witchcraft is woven through both local gatherings and digital connections, creating a vibrant tapestry that spans across the globe. In this age where technology meets tradition, the importance of fostering strong, supportive communities in witchcraft cannot be overstated. These communities serve as sanctuaries of knowledge, support, and shared experiences, helping each member to thrive not only in their personal practices but also in their spiritual journeys.

Online Communities and Connection

In recent years, the rise of online platforms has revolutionized the way witches connect and learn from each other. From forums and social media groups to dedicated witchcraft networks, these digital spaces offer invaluable resources for sharing knowledge, experiences, and support. For many, especially those in remote areas or in environments less accepting of witchcraft, online communities are a lifeline, providing connections that are both empowering and essential for personal growth.

Imagine you are a solitary practitioner seeking guidance on a particular spell or facing a spiritual dilemma. Through online platforms, you can connect with experienced practitioners who can offer advice, insights, and encouragement. These platforms often host a diverse range of discussions, from spellcraft and ritual work to more philosophical debates about the nature of magic itself. Moreover, for those who might feel isolated in their practices, these online connections affirm that they are part of a global, vibrant community that transcends geographical boundaries.

Local Covens and Gatherings

While digital platforms provide excellent avenues for connection, the power of face-to-face interactions remains unparalleled. Local covens and gatherings foster a sense of belonging and community that can be deeply transformative. Participating in rituals, celebrating sabbats, and simply sharing space with fellow practitioners can significantly enhance your practice, grounding your digital learning in the physical world.

Local gatherings also offer the tactile experiences of witchcraft—feeling the energy of a group ritual, crafting spells together, or sharing the quiet moments of a meditative circle. These experiences can forge deep bonds among practitioners, creating support networks that extend beyond magical practices into the realm of personal support and lifelong friendships. If you're new to an area or to witchcraft, reaching out to local metaphysical shops or searching online for nearby pagan or witchcraft groups can be a great start to finding your community.

Interfaith and Cross-Tradition Alliances

Beyond the internal community of witchcraft, building bridges with other spiritual and religious groups can enrich our practices and broaden our perspectives. Interfaith dialogues and cross-tradition alliances foster mutual respect and understanding, breaking down misconceptions and stereotypes while highlighting the common threads in our spiritual quests.

Such alliances can be particularly enlightening, as they expose us to different worldviews and practices, challenging us to think more deeply about our own beliefs and rituals. They can also be a source of support in broader societal contexts, where spiritual practices might still face misunderstanding and prejudice. By standing together, diverse spiritual communities can advocate more effectively for religious freedom and mutual respect.

Mentorship and Education

At the heart of community lies the transfer of knowledge—essential for the preservation and evolution of witchcraft. Mentorship connects the wisdom of experienced practitioners with the fresh energy of new seekers, ensuring that the rich traditions of witchcraft continue to thrive. Mentors can offer guidance, insight, and support, helping novices navigate their paths and avoid common pitfalls.

Education, too, is a vital component of community.

Workshops, classes, and informal teaching sessions help disseminate knowledge and skills that are crucial for the development of competent, ethical practitioners. These educational efforts help maintain the integrity of witchcraft practices, ensuring that they are passed on accurately and respectfully.

In fostering both mentorship and education within the witchcraft community, we ensure that our traditions— both old and new—are respected, preserved, and adapted responsibly for future generations. Whether through formal coven structures, informal mentorship relationships, or educational workshops, the nurturing of new practitioners enriches the entire community, weaving new threads into the fabric of our shared magical heritage.

8.3 INNOVATING SPELLCRAFT WITH MODERN TECHNOLOGY

As we continue to navigate through our increasingly digital era, the integration of technology in witchcraft is not just inevitable but also incredibly enriching. The realm of digital spellcasting and rituals, for instance, is expanding rapidly, offering new dimensions of engagement and experience that were once unimaginable. Consider the fascinating world of virtual reality (VR) and augmented reality (AR), which are beginning to find their way into magical practices. Imagine donning a VR headset and being transported to a digitally created sacred circle by the sea or an ancient forest at sunset, all from the comfort of your own home.

These VR rituals can offer immersive experiences that many might not otherwise have due to geographical, physical, or time constraints. Similarly, AR can bring a layer of magic into our everyday environments, allowing us to interact with digital elements superimposed onto our real-world settings. For example, you could cast a circle by simply pointing your smartphone around a room, watching as magical symbols and protective barriers appear on the screen, integrated seamlessly into your physical space.

The rise of apps designed specifically for witchcraft practices also marks a significant evolution in the way we approach our craft. These applications can track lunar phases, aligning our spellcasting and ritual timings with the celestial bodies. They can offer guided meditations that help in grounding and centering, incorporating binaural beats or guided imagery to enhance the spiritual experience. Imagine an app that not only reminds you of upcoming astrological shifts but also suggests personalized spells or rituals based on your astrological chart and current planetary alignments. Additionally, spellcasting apps can store your favorite spells and rituals, provide ingredient lists, and even guide you through spell steps, much like a cooking app does with recipes. This accessibility makes it easier for both beginners and seasoned practitioners to integrate witchcraft smoothly into daily life without the need to carry books or extensive notes.

Social media's role in modern witchcraft is another area where technology's impact is profoundly felt. Platforms like Instagram, TikTok, and YouTube have become valuable resources for sharing knowledge and connecting with other practitioners worldwide. Through these platforms, experienced witches can share videos that break down complex spells or rituals, offer tarot readings, or share experiences that help to demystify aspects of the craft that may seem inaccessible or secretive. For those in areas where witchcraft might still be viewed with suspicion or misunderstanding, social media offers a community and a sanctuary where beliefs and practices are not just accepted but celebrated. Moreover, the visual and interactive nature of social media platforms allows for a dynamic exchange of ideas and innovations, ensuring that witchcraft remains a living, evolving practice.

The incorporation of technological tools in ritual and spellwork, beyond digital platforms, is also enhancing traditional practices. Tools like electric candles, for instance, provide safer alternatives for indoor rituals without diminishing the symbolic power of candlelight. Electronic music devices can be used to play chants or ritual music, helping to set the mood and enhance the energy of the space. Even more innovative are tools like energy meters or apps that claim to detect and visualize the energy flow in a room, helping practitioners adjust their practices based on real-time feedback. These tools not only make the practice of witchcraft more adaptable to modern lifestyles but also invite a curious overlap between technology and spirituality, opening up new pathways for understanding and manipulating energy.

As we continue to explore these technological innovations, it becomes clear that they are not just conveniences but powerful enhancements that deepen our engagement with the craft. They bring witchcraft into the digital age, making it more accessible, understandable, and applicable in our daily lives. Through these innovations, we ensure that our ancient practices not only survive but thrive in a world that is ever-changing, continuously expanding the boundaries of what we might achieve with our magic.

8.4 THE GLOBAL WITCH: WITCHCRAFT WITHOUT BORDERS

Modern witchcraft is vibrant and varied, woven from threads of numerous cultures and traditions from around the globe. As we continue to connect and interact on an unprecedented scale, the opportunities for cross-cultural exchange in our craft have expanded dramatically. This exchange, when approached with respect and openness, enriches our practices and broadens our horizons, allowing us to share and learn from a kaleidoscope of magical traditions. However, this interaction also presents challenges, particularly in navigating cultural sensitivities and avoiding the pitfalls of appropriation.

Imagine a scenario where you, as a practitioner, are introduced to a spell or ritual from a culture different from your own. The allure of expanding your magical repertoire is undeniable. Yet, this is a delicate dance of respect and understanding. It begins with education—taking the time to learn not just the method but the history, context, and significance of the practice within its original culture. Engaging with practitioners from that culture, if possible, can provide insights and nuances that books or online resources cannot capture. This respectful approach ensures that when you incorporate elements from other traditions, you do so in a way that honors their origins and meanings rather than reducing them to mere exotic novelties.

The celebration of global rituals and festivals offers a vivid illustration of how shared magical experiences can unite practitioners across the world. Consider the potent energy of global celebrations like the Solstices, which are recognized and revered in various forms across many cultures. Participating in these global rituals, perhaps through synchronized ceremonies or shared online rituals, not only deepens your personal practice but also connects you with witches worldwide. These shared experiences foster a sense of unity and collective power, reinforcing the idea that although we may follow different paths, we are connected by the universal currents of magical practice.

In our increasingly interconnected world, witchcraft faces the imperative to adapt and respond to global challenges such as climate change, social justice issues, and the need for healing on both a personal and planetary scale. Witchcraft, inherently tied to the rhythms and health of the Earth, positions us uniquely to influence and contribute positively to these global issues. For instance, incorporating eco-magic into your practice, focusing spells and rituals on healing the Earth, or using your magical practice to raise awareness and energy for social justice causes integrates your spiritual practice with activism. This adaptation not only enhances the relevance of witchcraft in addressing contemporary issues but also empowers you as a practitioner to act on your convictions and influence real-world change.

The role of the internet in this global expansion of witchcraft cannot be overstated. As a tool, it has revolutionized how we connect, learn, and practice. Online platforms and social media have broken down geographical barriers, making witchcraft accessible to those in remote or isolated locations and creating spaces for practitioners to share, learn, and collaborate effortlessly. Through the internet, rituals, spells, and teachings can be shared in real-time, tutorials can be accessed at the click of a button, and support from the global witch community can be sought and given, making the practice of witchcraft an inclusive and shared experience across cultures and continents.

This digital connectivity also allows for the preservation and sharing of magical knowledge in ways that were not possible before. Digital archives, online libraries, and virtual gatherings ensure that the wisdom of the craft is preserved for future generations and that the rich diversity of witchcraft traditions is celebrated and maintained. As you continue to navigate your path in witchcraft, consider how these tools might enhance not only your practice but also your connection to the global witch community, enriching your craft with the diverse energies and perspectives that make our community so uniquely powerful.

8.5 PERSONALIZING YOUR PRACTICE FOR THE NEXT GENERATION

In a world that is rapidly evolving, the personalization of your witchcraft practice is not just a journey of self-expression but a necessary adaptation to remain relevant and resonant. The key to this evolution lies in continually aligning your magical practices with your growing understanding of the world and your place within it. As you navigate changes—both in the broader cultural landscape and in your personal life—your practice must also shift and grow. This is not about abandoning the core principles or traditions that have shaped your path but rather about allowing your practice to be a living, breathing reflection of who you are in the present moment.

Consider the ways in which you can infuse new life into your rituals and spells. This might involve incorporating new symbols that have become meaningful to you, adapting rituals to include new elements that resonate with your current life phase or even rewriting spells from a fresh perspective that better suits your evolved understanding. For instance, if you find deeper resonance with water elements as you grow older, consider how you can shift your practice to include more rituals by the water or using water-based elements. This personalization not only keeps your practice vibrant and effective but also ensures that it remains a true reflection of your spirit, adaptable and responsive to the ever-changing tides of life.

Creating a magical legacy, be it through your biological

family or your chosen family, is another profound aspect of personalizing your practice for future generations. This legacy goes beyond merely passing on knowledge; it is about instilling a sense of wonder, respect, and responsibility towards witchcraft and the natural world. Start by sharing your magical experiences and the lessons they've taught you. Whether it's through storytelling, creating a family grimoire, or involving your loved ones in your rituals, each act of sharing is a seed planted for the future. These seeds will grow into a forest of understanding and reverence for the magical arts, ensuring that the wisdom you've gained is preserved and expanded upon by those who follow.

Innovation within tradition is not just a challenge; it's an exciting opportunity to test the boundaries of what we consider possible within our craft. Encourage yourself and others in your community to experiment with new methodologies, perhaps integrating modern understandings of herbs, crystals, and energy work into traditional frameworks. For example, could a traditional protection spell be enhanced by understanding the conductive properties of certain metals or the frequency vibrations of crystals? By experimenting and innovating, you not only contribute to the growth of witchcraft as a practice but also ensure its relevance for new generations who might be looking for ways to connect their modern experiences with ancient wisdom.

Documentation and knowledge sharing are crucial in this age of information. As you evolve your practice, keep detailed records not just of what you do but of how you do it and why. Whether you prefer the tactile feel of pen on paper in your grimoire or a digital blog that reaches witches worldwide, the act of documenting your practice serves a dual purpose. It helps you reflect and refine your own practices, and it offers a valuable resource for others. In this digital era, consider sharing your journey online. Create blog posts, videos, or podcasts that discuss not only the successes but also the challenges and how you've overcome them. This transparency not only demystifies the practice for newcomers but also encourages a culture of continuous learning and sharing within the witchcraft community.

By taking these steps, you ensure that your witchcraft practice is not just a path you walk alone but a bridge connecting past, present, and future practitioners. This bridge, built from the stones of tradition and the mortar of innovation, stands as a testament to the living, evolving nature of our craft—a legacy of wisdom, wonder, and adaptation that will inspire generations to come. As you continue to personalize your practice, remember that each choice and change is a thread in the larger tapestry of the magical community, contributing to a vibrant, dynamic picture of modern witchcraft.

8.6 THE NEVER-ENDING JOURNEY OF LEARNING IN WITCHCRAFT

Witchcraft is not merely a set of rituals and spells; it is a dynamic and evolving path of learning that continues throughout your life. This perpetual journey is fueled by an ever-deepening curiosity and a commitment to personal growth. Each day offers new opportunities to expand your knowledge and refine your practice, whether through studying ancient traditions or exploring the latest scientific understandings that can inform your magical work.

The beauty of witchcraft lies in its fluidity—its ability to adapt and grow with each new piece of knowledge and every unique experience. As you continue to explore this magical path, you will discover that the learning never truly ends. There are always deeper layers to uncover and new perspectives to consider. This ongoing process is what keeps the practice of witchcraft vibrant and relevant. It encourages you not just to accumulate knowledge but to actively engage with it, to question, experiment, and integrate it into your daily practices.

Embracing new discoveries is crucial in keeping your practice alive and dynamic. The world around us is constantly changing, and with it, our understanding of the nature of reality, energy, and consciousness. Advances in fields like quantum physics, psychology, and ecology can provide profound insights into the forces at work in our spells and rituals. For instance, understanding the psychological impact of ritual on the human brain can help you design spells that are more effective, tapping into the deep power of the subconscious mind. Similarly, ecological knowledge can lead to more sustainable and harmonious practices that truly honor the Earth and its cycles.

Integrating modern scientific knowledge into your

witchcraft doesn't mean abandoning the mystical elements of the craft; rather, it enhances your understanding and deepens your connection to the magic you practice. It allows you to see the threads that connect the seen and unseen worlds, weaving them together in a tapestry that is both ancient and modern. This integration also encourages a more holistic approach to witchcraft, one that respects and utilizes all sources of knowledge to create a practice that is not only powerful but also informed and conscientious.

Personal experience, too, plays an irreplaceable role in your witchcraft journey. Each spell you cast, each ritual you perform, and each moment of connection with the divine is a learning experience that shapes and defines your path. These experiences are your most valuable teachers, offering lessons that are uniquely tailored to your personal journey. They help you understand not just the mechanics of witchcraft but also its heart and soul—how it feels to live a magical life and to see the world through the eyes of a witch.

Your personal experiences also offer invaluable insights into what works best for you in your practice. What feels most powerful and effective? What aligns best with your intentions and your values? These are questions that only your experiences can answer. They encourage you to trust in your own wisdom and intuition and to recognize that while books and teachers can offer guidance, the true knowledge of witchcraft is found within your own practice and your own heart.

As you continue on this never-ending path of learning, remember that each step forward is a step into greater understanding, not just of witchcraft, but of yourself and the universe. Keep your mind open and your heart willing to learn, and you will find that witchcraft is a lifelong journey of discovery that continually enriches your life.

~

IN CLOSING THIS CHAPTER, we reflect on the essence of witchcraft as a dynamic and evolving practice, deeply inter-twined with continuous learning and personal growth. As we move forward, these principles guide us not only in our magical practices but also in our daily lives, encouraging us to remain curious, open-minded, and ever-willing to grow. This journey of learning is not just about acquiring knowl-edge; it's about transforming ourselves and, by extension, the world around us. Let us carry with us the commitment to lifelong learning and the relentless pursuit of wisdom, which are the true marks of the wise witch.

If you enjoyed this book, please consider leaving a review.

AFTERWORD

As we come to the close of this journey together, I hope you feel a renewed sense of empowerment and capability within your own life. This book has been crafted not just as a guide, but as a companion to accompany you as you weave magic into the very fabric of your daily existence.

Throughout these pages, we've explored how modern witchcraft can serve as a profound tool for personal growth, self-care, and empowerment. By integrating these practices into your daily life, you're not just performing spells—you're embarking on a transformative path that encourages a deeper connection with the energies that flow around and within you.

We have taken great care to respect and honor cultural traditions, emphasizing the importance of navigating our practice with mindfulness and appreciation. This commitment to cultural sensitivity and inclusivity is crucial, as it enriches our practice and ensures it remains a force for positive impact in our diverse world.

The practical, adaptable nature of the spellwork presented here is designed to fit seamlessly into your busy lifestyle. Remember, each spell and ritual can be modified to suit your personal needs and circumstances. The use of accessible ingredients underscores our goal: to make witchcraft an attainable part of your life, regardless of your daily demands or resources.

Ethical considerations have been a cornerstone of our discussions. As you continue to explore the enchanting realm of witchcraft, always remember the importance of consent, the impact of your actions, and the responsibility we hold to do no harm. These ethical guidelines are not just rules but are principles that help cultivate a practice rooted in respect and love.

I encourage you to keep learning, growing, and adapting your practice. Witchcraft is a dynamic and ever-evolving journey, not a destination. Each day offers new opportunities to deepen your understanding and refine your craft. Embrace this perpetual growth, and let it inspire a lifelong pursuit of knowledge and magical mastery.

Integrating witchcraft into your daily routines can transform mundane activities into moments of deep magical connection. Let the magic you've discovered infuse your everyday life with wonder and purpose. Whether it's a morning ritual to start your day with intention or a simple spell woven into your cooking routines, find joy in these small acts of enchantment.

Community engagement is also vital. Whether online or in person, connecting with fellow practitioners can greatly enhance your experience and provide essential support. Share your knowledge, learn from others, and find strength in the collective wisdom of the witchcraft community.

Now, as a call to action, I urge you to use the spells, rituals, and insights from this book as tools for your empowerment. Let them guide you in manifesting your desires, achieving your personal growth, and embracing your inner power.

In closing, my hope is that this book serves not only as a guide but as a source of inspiration for you. May it be a lantern in the dark, a companion in solitude, and a spark for your inner magic. Continue to explore, to dream, and to grow within the boundless realm of modern witchcraft. Here's to your journey—may it be magical, transformative, and profoundly empowering.

With all my warmth and blessings, Cerridwen

BIBLIOGRAPHY

- Bryjaimea. (n.d.). The Ethics of Witchcraft: Navigating Responsibility and ... [Blog post]. Retrieved from https://bryjaimea.com/articles/spirituality/ethics-of-witchcraft/
- Finnar Journal. (n.d.). Magical Technology in Contemporary Fantasy [Journal article]. Retrieved from https://journal.finfar.org/articles/magical-technology-in-contemporary-fantasy/
- Native Governance Center. (2023). Cultural Appropriation and Wellness Guide [PDF]. Retrieved from https://nativegov.org/wp-content/uploads/2023/01/Cultural-Appropriation-and-Wellness-Guide.pdf
- Nofi, J. (2022, July 20). 14 Self-Care Rituals to Practice Now. *Psychology Today*. https://www.psychologytoday.com/us/blog/the-empowerment-diary/202207/14-self-care-rituals-practice-now
- Britannica. (n.d.). Witchcraft - Paganism, Rituals, Beliefs. *Encyclopædia Britannica*. Retrieved from https://www.britannica.com/topic/witchcraft/Contemporary-witchcraft#:~:text=Contemporary%20witchcraft,-Wicca%20is%20a&text=Adherents%20of%20Wicca%20-worship%20the,solstice%2C%20and%20the%20vernal%20equinox.
- Naturally Modern Life. (n.d.). A Guide to Ethically Sourcing Crystals [Blog post]. Retrieved from https://naturallymodernlife.com/a-guide-to-ethically-sourcing-crystals/
- The Rose Craft. (n.d.). How to Make and Use a Grimoire [Blog post]. Retrieved from https://therosecraft.com/blogs/the-rose-pages/how-to-make-and-use-a-grimoire

BIBLIOGRAPHY

- Moody Moons. (2018, March 2). 20 Common Household Items Used in Witchcraft [Blog post]. Retrieved from https://www.moodymoons.com/2018/03/02/20-common-household-items-use-witchcraft/

- Shamans Market. (n.d.). Understanding Phases of the Moon and Rituals for ... [Blog post]. Retrieved from https://www.shamansmarket.com/blogs/musings/moon-phases-assist-personal-growth

- Naturally Modern Life. (n.d.). Beginner Shadow Work for the Modern Witch [Blog post]. Retrieved from https://naturallymodernlife.com/beginner-shadow-work-for-the-modern-witch/

- Murphy, K. (n.d.). 9 Herbs to Enhance Intuition. *Kate Murphy*. Retrieved from https://www.thisiskatemurphy.com/post/9-herbs-to-enhance-intuition

- Dazed Beauty. (2022, May 20). Is it ever ethical to cast a love spell? Witches weigh in. *Dazed Digital*. https://www.dazeddigital.com/beauty/article/58140/1/is-it-ethical-to-cast-a-love-spell-witches-weigh-in

- Gelardi, L. (2020, October 30). A Modern Witch's Guide to Casting Love Spells. *Allure*. https://www.allure.com/story/how-to-cast-love-spells

- Dazed Beauty. (2022, May 20). Is it ever ethical to cast a love spell? Witches weigh in. *Dazed Digital*. https://www.dazeddigital.com/beauty/article/58140/1/is-it-ethical-to-cast-a-love-spell-witches-weigh-in

- All Crystal. (n.d.). 9 Best Ways to Cast Spells for Emotional Healing with ... *All Crystal*. Retrieved from https://www.allcrystal.com/articles/emotional-healing-spells/

- Processing Foundation. (2018, June 14). Portal.Web: An Intro to Cyber Witch Practices. *Medium*. https://medium.com/processing-foundation/portal-web-an-intro-to-cyber-witch-practices-6b3322969366

- Zakroff, L. T. (2019). *Weave the Liminal: Living Modern Traditional Witchcraft*. Barnes & Noble.

- Henriques, M. (2023, September 12). Ethical Considerations in Spellcasting. *The Stardust Club*. https://medium.com/the-stardust-club/ethical-considerations-in-spellcasting-243899e325aa

- Wenson, R. (2022, February 8). Digital Witchcraft 101. *Medium*. https://medium.com/@rebeccawenson/digital-witchcraft-101-26ad0032dd2f

- Spells8. (n.d.). Magical Substitutions: Herbs, Candles and Spell Ingredients. *Spells8*. Retrieved from https://spells8.com/herbs-substitutions-witchcraft/

- Eileen, S. (2020, September 1). Ethical Baneful Magic for all Skill and Experience Levels. Retrieved from https://sidneyeileen.com/2020/09/01/ethical-baneful-magic-for-all-skill-and-experience-levels/

- Faena, A. (n.d.). 5 Steps to Creating A Talisman (To Transform Superstition ... Retrieved from https://www.faena.com/aleph/5-steps-to-creating-a-talisman-to-transform-superstition-to-magic

- Cornell Botanic Gardens. (n.d.). The Supernatural Side of Plants. Retrieved from https://cornellbotanicgardens.org/the-supernatural-side-of-plants-2/

- Earth Monk. (n.d.). Psychic protection for empaths. Retrieved from https://earthmonk.guru/psychic-protection-for-empaths/

- Cooglife. (2019, February). Modern witchcraft as a form of self-care, empowerment. Retrieved from http://cooglife.com/2019/02/modern-witchcraft-as-a-form-of-self-care-empowerment/

- Google Arts & Culture. (n.d.). Magic in the Ancient World. Retrieved from https://artsandculture.google.com/story/magic-in-the-ancient-world-isac-museum/EgURzJZdqxZrJQ?hl=en

- Jaimea, B. (n.d.). The Ethics of Witchcraft: Navigating Responsibility and ... Retrieved from https://bryjaimea.com/articles/spirituality/ethics-of-witchcraft/

- Spells 8. (n.d.). Magical Substitutions: Herbs, Candles and Spell Ingredients. Retrieved from https://spells8.com/herbs-substitutions-witchcraft/
- Wishful, 1. (n.d.). Ethics and Accountability in Witchcraft: Nurturing Integrity ... Retrieved from https://medium.com/@wishful11984/ethics-and-accountability-in-witchcraft-nurturing-integrity-and-healthy-practices-a6ac9f286210
- ReligionLink. (n.d.). Spiritual technologies: Exploring the intersections between religion and modern tech. Retrieved from https://religionlink.com/source-guides/spiritual-technologies-exploring-the-intersections-between-religion-and-modern-tech/
- Wishful, M. (n.d.). Intersectionality and Diversity: Fostering Equity and Support in the Witchcraft Community. Medium. https://medium.com/@wishful11984/intersectionality-and-diversity-fostering-equity-and-support-in-the-witchcraft-community-eb59a3ccdf63
- Blaspheme Boutique. (n.d.). Eco-Witchcraft: Embracing Environmentally Friendly Practices in the Craft. Retrieved from https://blasphemeboutique.com/blogs/news/eco-witchcraft-embracing-environmentally-friendly-practices-in-the-craft

Made in United States
Orlando, FL
17 June 2025